UNFIN[illegible] BUSINESS

Nine Laws for Acceleration

GARY KEESEE

Unfinished Business: Nine Laws for Acceleration

ISBN: 978-1-945930-98-0

Faith Life Now
P.O. Box 779
New Albany, OH 43054
1-(888)-391-LIFE

You can reach Faith Life Now Ministries on the Internet at www.faithlifenow.com.

TABLE OF CONTENTS

INTRODUCTION

"Why aren't you up there?" That is what I heard the Lord say to me as I sat at the annual sales convention watching the top 10 sales leaders get their recognition, which by the way included a $100,000 bonus check. I was a little shocked when I heard that. I said, "Lord, you know why I am not up there; you called me to start and pastor a church for you. You know I am busy, really busy. These guys up on stage do this all day long. It is what they eat and breathe all year long to get here. I am a full-time pastor and really only work in my company on a part-time to spare time basis." Then I heard Him answer me, "I want you up there. It is a great opportunity for you to represent me here." Well, of course, I would have loved to be up there; who wouldn't? So, I said, "Well, Lord, I am already maxed out in my time, so you will have to show me what I need to do to make it possible, because right now I do not see that."

To give you a bit of history, at this point in my life, besides pastoring a large church of 3,500 people, I had been working in the financial industry selling insurance, securities, and helping people get out of debt for the previous 34 years. The convention I was attending was being put on by one of the many vendors that my financial company uses in helping my clients with their financial plans. I had used this particular vendor for the previous 14 years and usually did enough production to qualify to attend their annual event but at that point had never made the top tier.

My usual production was about 4 million a year, which put me in the top 200 offices out of 5,000 offices, so I did not feel too bad about my performance, especially since I was so busy. To get in the top 10 offices, I would have had to be doing over 10 million a year in production, and it was already March as I sat in this convention. I had no idea how I could ever reach the 10 million production level before the end of the year. Remember, I had been doing about 4 million in production a year for the previous 14 years!

But Drenda and I agreed that if the Lord was wanting us up there, then it must be possible—yet we had no idea, at that moment, how it could happen. I was preaching four services a weekend, traveling around 75 nights a year doing conferences, doing a daily TV broadcast, managing 75 employees, and running my financial company. Drenda was also doing her own daily TV broadcast. Add on top of that our five children and grandkids, and you have a pretty full life. Drenda and I sowed a financial seed and asked God to show us how to do what seemed to us the impossible.

To make a long story short—or I should say, to introduce a long story—the next spring, we were on that platform being recognized in the top tier, and yes, we received the $100,000 bonus check as well as a trip to Bora Bora! It was awesome and amazing. To go a step further, we made this top production level for the next six years straight. This was all done without using a new marketing plan, no added employees, no added overhead, no purchased leads. In fact, we did no advertising or marketing in any of those six years. So how did I go from 4 million in production for 14 straight years to over 10 million in production in less than 10 months and maintain a production level of between 12 and 15 million for the next five years? Again, it was not the result of attending a sales meeting or a conference on selling.

This change was a result of a dream I had where the Lord gave me the key that changed my financial life. This book is now being written six years later as a result of a second dream I had where the Lord was telling me to write this book. In that dream, I saw this book's title and the book's chapters as clearly as if I was holding the book in my hand.

Like me, I know that you want to win, take territory, and let God use you as a picture of His greatness. If that is your heart, then this book is for you. It is time to accelerate your success with these nine laws for acceleration. Let's not leave any unfinished business behind. When I go on to heaven, I want to know I accomplished my assignment, not just survived but thrived, by the grace of God. I want Him to shine through my life, showing people that the impossible is always possible!

—Gary Keesee

CHAPTER 1

WHERE DO YOU WANT TO GO?

The earth is a big place! There are a lot of fantastic places to visit and see, but strangely, so many people never get there. A recent survey that I read in *Forbes* magazine stated the following:

- Eleven percent of survey respondents have never traveled outside of the state where they were born.
- Over half of those surveyed (54 percent) say they've visited 10 states or fewer.
- As many as 13 percent say they have never flown in an airplane.
- Forty percent of those questioned said they've never left the country.
- Over half of respondents have never owned a passport. (Remember, for years you did not need one to travel to Canada, which may explain this large number.)[1]

I did find these numbers very interesting. But the following information obtained from the same survey is what I really found amazing: 85 percent of those surveyed said they had a desire to travel, and over 60 percent already had a list of the places that they would someday love to visit. When asked why they did not travel when they admitted they wanted to, their answer was simple: They

1. Lea Lane, "Percentage of Americans Who Never Traveled Beyond the State Where They Were Born? A Surprise," https://www.forbes.com, May 5, 2019

did not have the money they needed to travel. So, do you know what happens then? Nothing! You become an observer, a bystander in life. That is how I grew up.

My family never traveled when I grew up. I barely even knew the names of my neighboring towns, much less knew where they were and how to get there. To give you an illustration of just how dysfunctional I was in regard to travel, I will tell you of an event that took place when I was 14.

I grew up in the country surrounded by farmland in the middle of Ohio. My grandpa was a farmer, and my parents had built a home on a few acres of his farm, which I loved because there was a big pond next to our house. There was also a creek that ran from our pond into the woods, which is where I learned to trap and hunt. I spent so many days fishing and hiking around those woods! I just loved living out there. Although my hometown was only a few miles from the Columbus city limits, I never liked going into the big city much.

Well, this particular year, my friend and I decided to buy Schwinn bikes. Not just any old Schwinn bikes but 10-speeds with a real speedometer on them. Being too young to drive yet, I thought that bicycle was really something special. I saved up my money, and my friend and I both bought a brand-new Schwinn 10-speed. We would ride those bikes up and down our road and would also ride the mile and a half to school as well.

One day, we decided that we wanted to really go somewhere, a real trip on our new bikes. We grabbed a few dollars and headed down the road. About a mile from my house, we came to the first intersection. I knew that if I took a left, it would take me to school. I also knew that if I took a right, I would end up at the county line, which was about a mile and a half from that intersection. But I did not know where it went after you passed the county line; I had never gone that way before. Well, my friend did not know what came after the county line either, so we thought, *Let's go right and find out what is out there.* So that is what we did: we headed right, toward the county line and thought we were so grown-up and brave to launch out into the unknown.

We rode for a while, passed the county line, and kept on going. I remember thinking while we passed the county line, *Wow, we are really going somewhere now, a real trip.* As we continued on, we saw a small town ahead of us. We had no idea what town it was. As we got closer to the town, we spotted a little general store, and since it was a hot day and we were thirsty, we pulled into the parking lot and went inside to get a drink. We both went in and purchased our drink of choice. At that time in my life, that would have been a Mountain Dew. Oh, by the way, if you are a younger reader, that was a bottle, not a can, and was made with real sugar, not corn syrup. It was the best!

As we were paying for it, we told the lady at the cash register all about our bicycle trip we were taking and asked her what the name of the town was that we were at. When she told us, neither of us had ever heard of it before, so we asked her how far we were from that intersection back in New Albany. I remember how stupid I felt when she said it was five miles back. Five miles? That was it? We had only traveled five miles? We felt like it had to be at least 50! Although we realized that we had not gone far, we decided that we had ridden enough for one day, turned around, rode back to the intersection, and went home. That was a big trip for me. Can you imagine not even knowing the name of the town that was only a few miles from your house, the house that you grew up in? Again, we just did not travel much.

I can still remember being 19 and driving down to the Ohio River to go fishing with a friend. After we tried fishing for a bit, a storm blew in, so we decided to head back home. I remember asking my friend if he would mind if we just drove across the Ohio River bridge and came right back so I could say that I had actually left the state of Ohio. That day was the first time I had ever been in Kentucky. Wow, what a sheltered life I had growing up. So much of it was awesome, but without realizing it, it also held me back.

You already know that I love the outdoors. The worst punishment you could give me growing up was to tell me I had to stay indoors. I lived outside! I started hunting when I was in sixth grade, not because my dad hunted but because when my grandpa died, I was rummaging around in his basement and found a cardboard box full of parts of an old 65-year-old shotgun. I asked my dad if I could have it, and he said I could, not ever thinking that I could piece together a complete gun from that box of what he thought was junk, but I did. I think he was a little shocked the day I brought that gun out to him, showed him that I had fixed it, and asked him if he could shoot it for me to see if it really worked. I was surprised—let me rephrase that to shocked—that he said yes. I can remember that event like it was yesterday.

He found some old 12-gauge shotgun shells that he had. I had no idea why he had them since he did not own a gun. In those days, the shells were made of paper, unlike the plastic ones today. We went out behind the house, and he set a can up on a stick, stepped back about 40 yards, and fired the gun. He shot it a couple of times then invited me to shoot it. After that, he told me since I had put it together, it was mine to own, but I could not shoot it unless he gave me permission. I remember I thought my dad was so brave to pull that trigger. I still have that gun today.

That gun opened a new world to me. It was fall, and hunting season had just opened. A couple of my friends at school were talking about going rabbit hunting, and since I then had my own shotgun, I so wanted to try it. My dad surprised me in an even bigger way that fall. I began to talk to him about my interest in hunting rabbits, and he told me I could try it. I was in shock!

We lived in the country, and no one was really living around us at that time. My dad said I could go out behind our house on my grandpa's farm by myself! He explained to me that the rabbits liked to live along the fence rows, told me that it was also quail season, and reminded me that they were also back there. That afternoon, I bagged one rabbit and one quail. I was forever hooked on hunting!

I subscribed to any hunting magazine I could subscribe to. I had *Outdoor Life*, *Sports Afield*, *Field & Stream*, *Fur-Fish-Game*, and a few others. I would read every story in them with fascination. Back in that day, we did not have a Cabela's sporting goods store or a Walmart around, but we had Herter's catalog. It was equivalent to today's Cabela's catalog and would capture my imagination with all the cool things it carried. I would carry mine to school and look through it during study hall.

But here is the crippling part of the story; here is the point I want to make. Those magazines came to my house every single month all through middle school, all through high school, and continued during the next four years while I was out of high school living at home and working for my dad. Not once did I ever think, *I am going to go to that place or that place and do what I saw in those magazines.* Not once! It never crossed my mind! Although I read those stories with extreme adoration and fascination, even after I bought my own car and had my own money, never did I ever have the thought to go and to be a part of what I was reading.

You may be thinking, *That is strange*; and when I look back on it now, I agree, that was strange. So why didn't I ever dream of actually doing all those things I read about, or actually go to the Rocky Mountains? After all, getting there was easy. Interstate 70 ran through Columbus and ran straight into Denver. But not once did I ever think of driving there. Why? That is the question that must be answered.

I never knew I could.

I did not say it was not possible. I said I never knew that "I" could. I know what you are thinking: *This guy is a little nuts, and maybe I have just wasted my money on this book.* Let me explain. In my mind, I never saw myself in the stories and pictures I was reading. Because my parents did not travel and money was tight growing up, I had learned to say no before I said yes. My "No Training" was so complete that I never even thought about it. In other words, I would dismiss the possibility of going as not being possible for me before I ever picked up the thought that it might be. I can completely understand the people who at the beginning of this chapter never went as well. Let me review the survey.

"Eighty-five percent of those surveyed said they had a desire to travel, and over sixty percent already had a list of the places that they would someday love to visit."

Stop everything! Eighty-five percent wanted to travel, and sixty percent already had the places they wanted to travel to written down? So why didn't they go? Oh, I know, the survey said money was the issue. Well, I say, "No, that was just an excuse; money was not the issue."

It is just like when I wanted to buy that brand-new Schwinn 10-speed. I wanted it, and I found a way to work part time to make the money to pay for it. Every time I thought of that bike,

I imagined me riding it and how great it was going to be. Like me, admiring all those places and experiences in those magazines, those survey respondents never saw themselves in the picture. If they would have, they would have made a way to get there.

Let's face it: I had the car, I had the money; and if money had been an issue, I could have camped in the state park for $5 a night. Sadly, I was 40 years of age when I first saw those Rocky Mountains. To say I was overwhelmed would be an understatement. But I can remember being there and thinking, *Why didn't I do this earlier?*

This book is called *Unfinished Business*. It is about going someplace that you should have already been to, but for the same reasons I never made it to the mountains, you have hesitated. Your no training said you could not afford it, or you did not know how to do it, or various other reasons you used to talk yourself into being ordinary and average. But I want to remind you what the Lord said to me in the introduction, "I want you in the top 10. I want you to get that $100,000 bonus check. I want people to see my greatness in you!"

My word to you is this: "Why not you?"

I think it is vital that before we get any further into this book, and before I start coaching you on how to accelerate your life and your goals, that you really take a moment and ask yourself this question:

"Where do I want to go?"

Before you start dumbing down your answer as you filter it through your own say no before you say yes training, let me clarify the question. I am not asking you how you are going to do it or how you are going to pay for it. I am simply asking you: "What do you want to do?" I know that what we have just covered may appear as a very simplistic exercise, but it sets the posture for everything that happens next and leads us to the next question I want to ask you:

"And how fast do you want to get there?"

In the 1800s, people did not have many travel options. The horse was it. If someone wanted to travel from the Missouri River to Sacramento, California, it would take 4 to 6 months to get there. The norm then was to travel in a group, called a wagon train, for safety and friendship. The wagon trains would only travel about 12 to 15 miles per day, which made traveling by wagon train a long and perilous journey. There were raging rivers and high mountains to cross, and, of course, there were Indians to contend with. From 1835 to 1855, 10,000 people died on the long journey, not from Indian attacks but from illness or accidents, and yes, some did die from Indian attacks, about 4 percent.[2]

Can you imagine picking up the latest wagon train sales brochure with all the glossy pictures, and then it says, "We have only lost 10,000 people over the last 20 years, and we are proud of our record of only losing 4 percent of those traveling to Indian attacks"? How many do you think would sign up for that? With those stats, you may think no one in their right mind would take such a trip, but you would be wrong. Hundreds of thousands took the trip. I think we can agree that it was a perilous journey, but why would they risk the journey? In a simple answer, they were looking for a better life, a new future. They were really no different than you, but they did have a strong desire for change, and that dream was bigger than any trouble they might encounter on the way.

The second best way to travel was by boat, and some in that era would have said it was the best as far as comfort went. I am talking about going through Panama; and no, I am not talking about the Panama Canal but Panama. You would take a ship down

2. "What Is the California Trail?" https://lisbdnet.com, February 6, 2022

the eastern side of the United States and Central America until you came to Panama. Then you would unload your belongings and carry them across the narrow part of Panama to the Pacific Ocean, then back onto another ship and on to California. That trip took four months.

Now, if for some reason you hated poisonous snakes and the thought of dying from malaria, or a host of other diseases that could kill you was not your cup of tea, then you could go around the tip of South America. However, most of the ships that tried that did not make it as there were horrible storms around Cape Horn.

That's it. These methods of travel I have just mentioned were the only options in the 1800s until the railroad was built and you could travel the transcontinental railway. That railroad was a real game changer. Instead of taking four months to travel from Missouri to California, a person could make it in a week! Let's stop and think about this—four months or a week? Which one would you take? I think the choice is obvious.

Then, of course, the automobile and modern freeways today reduce that travel time to 42 hours to cross the entire country. And modern jet travel reduces that down even further to 4 to 5 hours. So how do you want to go? Even though air travel is so fast, 50 to 60% of Americans do not fly even once a year. The average American flies 1 to 1.5 times a year.[3]

And, yes, if I wanted to get across the United States, I could go on my bicycle, which would take the average person about 65 days. Though I would not call that a means of travel but an adventure by choice.

But let me make my point here: Over half of the people in

---

3. Douglas Adolph, "How Many Times Does the Average American Fly in a Year?" https://www.quora.com, January 6, 2018

the nation are not flying once a year! They are still in the 1800s, traveling by car, boat, and bicycle. And that is fine if you have the time. And it seems they do have the time!

According to a recent survey, 50% of Americans spend five to six hours on their phones daily, not including work-related phone use. Another 22% spend between three to four hours a day on their phones.[4]

The question is, is this because they have time or no vision?

Let me talk about time here just for a minute. The above statistics show us how much time we are wasting in our daily lives. For some reason, we think we have all the time in the world, but we don't. We all have a very limited timeline on this planet to get things done. We all have a start and an end date for our lives. What happens in between those markers determines if we truly lived our lives with the right priorities and fulfilled our God-given assignments.

Right now, as you are reading this page, you are moving. The earth is rotating at 1,042 miles an hour, and the earth itself is moving around the sun at 67,000 miles an hour. Our solar system itself is spinning with the rotation of the Milky Way, our galaxy at 483,000 miles an hour. But yet, it feels as if you are not moving at all.[5] [6] [7]

You see, time does not exist without a stationary reference point. When you are flying at 36,000 feet in a modern-day jetliner, it feels as if you are not moving fast at all as you gaze at the landscape

4. L. Ceci, "Average Time Spent Daily on a Smartphone in the United States 2021," https://www.statista.com/statistics/1224510, February 25, 2022
5. Ethan Siegal, "How Fast Does the Earth Move?" www.bigthink.com, March 16, 2022
6. "How Fast Is the Earth Moving Around the Sun?" www.wtwshow.com
7. Andrew Fraknoi, "How Fast Are You Moving When You Are Sitting Still?" Foothill College & the Astronomical Society of the Pacific, https://nightsky.jpl.nasa.gov, spring 2007

slowly moving below you. But as you get lower and approach the airport, it seems you are speeding up and the land below you is moving faster. But you are not speeding up at all. You then have a new perspective by which to judge your speed. And as your plane comes over the threshold of the runway, you can easily sense that you are moving very fast.

And so it is in our lives. Without goals, without purpose, there is nothing to judge our progress by. Let me say it this way:

Without purpose, there is no urgency!

Purpose lays out the path and the passion to get somewhere. All of a sudden, driving the car on a 1,400-mile trip may seem inappropriate when our purpose demands a faster solution, like a plane. This book is all about acceleration, but this book is worthless unless you have a reference point that brings a clear demand for urgency to mark your progress.

PURPOSE LAYS OUT THE PATH AND THE PASSION TO GET SOMEWHERE.

The stats I just gave regarding phone use show me that most people do not have any urgency, no purpose or passion accelerating their lives into a grand future. For some reason, they are content to watch the Super Bowls of life as a spectator, to sit in front of the silver screen and watch a heart grabbing romance while never getting in the game for themselves or never enjoying a real kiss.

The real indicator of the health of your passion is to ask yourself what you are practicing. Let me say it this way: What you are practicing shows me where you are going. If you desire to be a great pianist, you are not going to waste five to six hours a day on your device. What I find is that most people have no urgency and pass up so many opportunities to really change their lives. Why?

Because they just do not see the opportunities.

Have you ever cooked a hamburger? I am sure you have. It's pretty easy to do. Well, McDonald's took that simple concept, cooking a hamburger, and made it into an empire. Have you ever had a better hamburger than the one that McDonald's makes? I am sure you have. But yet, they are currently in 120 nations and territories around the world and serve 68 million customers each day! They operate 36,899 restaurants worldwide employing more than 375,000 people.[8]

What about Subway? Everyone has made a sub sandwich, yet they currently have 42,431 stores in 108 countries.[9]

Uber was started in 2009, just 13 years ago, and in 2021 was worth 86 billion dollars. Uber was started by two guys who were not starting the company just so they could find a more convenient method for them to personally grab a ride. No, they started Uber with the mindset of starting a revolution in travel. They were in 80 countries in just 12 years![10]

How did these companies do this? Simply put, they never started out with a goal of just making a hamburger. Why do I mention these companies? Well obviously, you would have to agree that they were well aware of time and urgency. They had a plan.

Today, a young person will take a job at McDonald's just to make some part-time money. It is just a stepping stone to somewhere else, yet while there, they never stop to wonder and learn how McDonald's became what it is today. They should be

8. "How Many McDonald's Locations Are There in the World?", https://www.worldatlas.com

9. "SWOT Analysis of Subway | Subway Strengths and Weakness, Opportunities and Threat," https://biznewske.com, February 25, 2022

10. Dan Blystone, "The Story of Uber," https://www.investopedia.com/articles/personal-finance/111015/story-uber.asp, updated September 19, 2021

taking notes on how they do what they do and why. It might serve them better than a college education.

This is what happened to Cordia Harrington, a single mom of three boys who was working in real estate and trying to find a more stable field to work in. She thought buying a McDonald's franchise might give her more time to spend with her children. She ended up owning three. At the time, McDonald's was in the process of planning to open another bakery, and Cordia was put on the bun committee. Her assignment was to give her input on the buns that McDonald's served by the millions, how they tasted and how they made them. She took lots of notes.

Although she was working to help McDonald's with their bun project, she was secretly taking notes for herself. She felt she could build a better bakery than what McDonald's was looking at. She presented her plans to McDonald's, and they rejected it. But four years later and after 32 interviews, they decided that they would buy their buns from her. The problem was she did not have a bakery yet and she had to borrow the money to build one, which she said almost took her under. Well, to make a long story short, the buns you are eating today at McDonald's, Chili's, Ruby Tuesday's, KFC, and Pepperidge Farm were baked at her bakery, the Tennessee Bun Company. It is known as the fastest automated bakery in the world, delivering 9 million baked goods daily for 1,500 customers. Yes, you read that right![11]

These stories just do not happen, as you know. It took hard work and a vision to succeed. I think you would have to agree that she had passion and urgency about her dream. She was not going to be wasting time. So, let's circle back to the reason you picked this book up. Let's go back to that very first question.

---

11. Tatiana Morales, "How She Became 'The Bun Lady,'" cbsnews.com, May 18, 2005

Where do you want to go?

The real answer to this question can be summed up with the word—want. Where do you "want" to go? In the past, your no before yes training had you confined to a life of survival and mediocrity. But now, you have a choice. Let's get those *Outdoor Life* magazines back out and reread the stories, except this time realize that you can do that, you can go there. Put yourself in the picture. Let yourself dream!

CHAPTER 2

SLAVES DON'T DREAM DREAMS!

I trust you have thought more about what I said in the previous chapter regarding where you want to go. It seems that people run around in circles, and at the end of the day—like a hamster on a hamster wheel—they stop, tired from all the running, then look and find that they have traveled nowhere. This book is about acceleration, and the beginning of that whole process is having a direction set before you start out. Of course, I realize that many times, we do not know where we want to go. Again, I believe that is because of our say no before we say yes training. We do not allow ourselves to dream or, as I said previously, to see ourselves in that glossy picture, to imagine ourselves in our future.

When Drenda and I were in horrible debt and I was on antidepressants and was having panic attacks, I really did not think much about where I wanted to go. I didn't care. I just wanted to survive one more week. My goal was just to be able to pay the rent one more time, buy groceries, and pay my utilities before they cut off my electricity. This is the stress that so many people live with; they are one paycheck away from being homeless. There is no security in that. The Bible mentions this in the book of Proverbs.

> *The rich rule over the poor, and the borrower is slave to the lender.*
>
> —Proverbs 22:7

Slaves do not dream dreams; their dream is to stop, not to go. Slaves do not have options. They are told what to do. I am sure you have probably heard the cry of modern-day slavery: "I have to go to work." It is said that over 80% of Americans do not like their jobs, and 33% actually hate them.[12] The reason? They are like square pegs in round holes; they don't fit. They are not taking jobs out of passion for what they will be doing. They are taking jobs to make a paycheck, with a mindset of survival. Because of that, we are emotionally sick.

Have you ever heard someone say, "Darn, I have to go fishing today"? I doubt it. They get to go fishing. Wouldn't it be great if you loved your occupation as much as your hobby, if you could say, "I can't wait for Monday"? Again, for most people, this is not the reality of their lives. But this is how God made you to function. He gave you unique talents and abilities and created you to succeed in your passion and purpose. Paying the bills has replaced vision for most people. Slavery is now the American way of life, with debt hijacking our freedom and causing us to give up on our dreams.

If you know my story from reading my other books, then you will remember I lived like this for nine years—nine years of living in financial hell. I was living as if I was an orphan with no father and no home. Everything was insecure. The pile of bills was huge, and the daily phone calls trying to collect from me what I did not have were nonstop. I had borrowed from my parents, my wife's parents, pawnshops, and anyone I could borrow from. I had 10 maxed out credit cards, IRS liens, finance company loans, car payments, and back rent. It got so bad that fear overtook my life, and I was even afraid to leave my house. I will admit there were many times, before I knew better, that I would ask the question,

12. Ken Keis, Ph.D., "Why Do People Hate Their Jobs?" Linkedin.com, October 6, 2014

"Where is God in all this?"

When people hear our story, they many times will say, "Well, it was a good thing that you came to Christ through all that." But most do not understand that Drenda and I were already Christians when all this was going on. I had a BA in Old Testament theology and a year of Bible college under my belt. We attended a great church where I heard God's promises on a weekly basis, but something was wrong, terribly wrong. We were living in an old 1853 farmhouse at the time. Everything was broken. We found the carpet in the boys' room along the road. Their mattresses were found in a nursing home's discard pile. Our appliances were over 20 years old, and our cars barely ran.

Every day was a day of financial stress and pressure. I worked hard in my sales position, but all I managed to do was barely survive until I finally hit bottom. I was out of options with no more money from family; no more pawnshop loans, as there was nothing left to pawn; and no more credit available. I had just gotten off the phone with an attorney who was threatening to sue me, and for the first time, I realized I was done. There was no way of escape this time.

In tears, I climbed the stairs, laid across my bed, and cried out to God for help. I had no idea what to do. I know what you are thinking: *You mean you waited nine years before you asked God for help?* No, of course not. But this time, I was empty. No more Gary Keesee was left to come up with another self-made solution. All those years, I was still leaning to the world's system to carry me through. But now, there was nothing. As I laid across my bed in tears, crying out to Him, it was from my heart. I had to hear from Him. He was my only hope. And just like that, I heard His voice. It was not audible, but it almost sounded like it was. He told me that the reason I was in this mess was because I had never taken the time to learn how His Kingdom worked.

I will have to admit that I really had no clue what He meant by that. As I said, I had five years of schooling to learn how His Kingdom worked; didn't I? But the word Kingdom stuck with me. What did He mean by that? It was not a word that I used often. But one thing was for sure: I was going to find out what He meant that day. I went straight downstairs to Drenda. We held hands and prayed that God would show us what He meant, and we repented for making such a mess of our finances. Well, to make a long story short, He began to teach us what He meant, and it totally changed our entire lives.

By applying what He showed me, we were able to get completely out of debt in two and a half years. He showed us how to launch several new companies, and we began to prosper in a way that I had never even thought possible. We went on to build and pay for our dream home on over 55 beautiful acres. We had beautiful new stainless steel appliances, hardwood floors, crown molding, and over 7,000 square feet of space for our family and offices to run my business from. I cannot tell you how thrilled we were to see the Kingdom work in our lives. We began paying cash for our cars and anything else we needed. We were free. The greatest change was that we were able to be generous and begin supporting the Kingdom of God as He led us. We were able to stop thinking of our giving in terms of hundreds of dollars and instead think in terms like hundreds of thousands of dollars.

To be sure, our lives drastically changed. But probably one, if not the biggest, of the changes I saw was that Drenda and I were able to dream again. Not just dreams of paying the next month's mortgage payment on time but dreams of purpose for our lives. We wanted to help people learn what we learned, how we got free.

By the way, if you are interested in hearing our entire story and what God taught us about the Kingdom, I have written a series of five books called the "Your Financial Revolution" series. I would strongly suggest you get these five books. Remember, I was in debt and hopeless for nine long years, yet today I am a millionaire. That just did not happen; we are not that good. You need to find out how that happened and all that God showed Drenda and me. So, get a copy of the books. They will teach you how the Kingdom of God operates through laws and principles that you will need to know. Take it from someone who has been there, got the T-shirt, and wishes they never did. The good news is that you do not have to go there either. Consider getting the entire set at garykeesee.com.

Okay, enough about my books. Let me circle back to the reason I even went down that rabbit trail. I made a statement at the beginning of this chapter where I said that when Drenda and I were living with serious debt, I never thought about where I was going. We were so busy saying no to everything that there was no room for yes! So, I completely understand if you currently have no idea where you are going or should be going, but I know you would like to find that direction—and you need to find it. So, let me tell you a simple statement that Drenda and I have said for years:

YOU WILL NEVER DISCOVER WHO YOU REALLY ARE AND WHAT YOU WERE CREATED TO BE UNTIL YOU FIX THE MONEY THING.

"You will never discover who you really are and what you were created to be until you fix the money thing."

Until you fix your money thing, you are basically a slave to survival. As I said earlier, slaves do not have great dreams. They have their noses to the grindstone for someone else. Their dream is to stop, not go. Vision requires provision; provision is provision. I know, a little play on words. Think about it. Provision is pro–vision. Slaves do not have vision. They just do what they are told. So, the best thing you can do to start finding out where you want to go is to start getting your finances in order and get out of debt.

Once Drenda and I got out of debt, wow, we had all kinds of ideas in regard to what we could and wanted to do. We launched a church, we went on daily TV, we built multimillion dollar facilities, and launched schools. We wrote books and then translated them into dozens of languages to reach people with the good news of the Kingdom of God all over the world. We have never stopped having ideas. And so will you as you start learning how God's Kingdom works, you start dreaming, and stop being an observer in life. Start seeing yourself in the picture.

As I said in the introduction, this book came about from a dream I had in 2016. In the dream, I saw this book, I saw the chapters, and the title. God told me to write this book about the nine laws for acceleration that He taught me. In the dream, I understood that God wanted me to write it to help His businesspeople capture what they were called to capture. Now, don't get me wrong. This book is for anyone and everyone. But in the dream, I sensed that although God had given many of His people an idea and vision for a business, they were not capturing all of the potential from their business that God had intended for them to have. And He said that these businesspeople knew they should be doing better and were frustrated because they weren't. He said they knew there was more but were not sure how to reach it, and this book was going to be written to help them get there! You may say, "Well, you had the dream in 2016, and this is 2022. Why so long?" Good question. I prayed about that all these years since 2016, and I never had the go-ahead from the Spirit of God to write it. Instead, I felt I was to finish my five-book Your Financial Revolution series first, because it does not matter how great these nine laws for acceleration are. You will need to understand the Kingdom to take full advantage of them.

The concepts and revelation in this book started in prayer on the morning of September 9, 2009. I was teaching at a church in Alabama the evening before this event occurred. It was a good meeting, but I was in turmoil. The financial crash had occurred in 2008 and was still going on in 2009, and I had some big issues I was facing. Our campus, which we call the Now Center, was originally a 5.2 million-dollar project, which consisted of a loan from our bank and 2.5 million dollars of our own cash we had saved. The builder was a friend of my family, having framed our personal home several years earlier. Well, you might remember that commodity prices skyrocketed in 2008 and 2009. Our steel prices for the Now Center went up 300 percent over bid, asphalt went so high that it became cheaper to use cement, oil was $140 a barrel, and so on.

Well, those price increases put us about one million over budget. Since we were already in the midst of the project and almost finished, the bank said that providing the extra million was no problem; and they gave us a line of credit for the additional million dollars.

You might remember the huge number of foreclosures there were during that time and how the banks found themselves in serious trouble. In fact, the banking system almost collapsed. I never heard anything from our bank during this crisis, and I thought since our loans were already established and we had made every payment on time that we had nothing to worry about. But the day that I picked up our local paper and saw on the front page that our bank had just laid off 550 people and had stopped lending, I was no longer sure. Sure enough, they called and said that they were pulling our line of credit.

The real problem was that the builder, our friend, had already spent the million dollars, counting on that line of credit to take care of that. I can remember the day that he came by to pick up his million dollars, and we had to tell him that the bank had pulled that money and we just did not have it yet. He was rather shocked and concerned as he still had to pay all of his vendors and his own staff as well. But as a believer, he knew that we both needed to pray about it and believe God for an answer. So, when I was in Alabama, as I woke up the morning after the previous night's meeting, I began to pray again about this situation.

It was also during this same season that God had spoken to me to start doing a television outreach teaching about His Kingdom. Well, I did not know anything about TV except that it was very expensive, and I had no idea how I would find the $300,000 needed to do that on top of everything else I was facing. When God led me to start doing TV, He made it very clear that He was going to bring the funds to do that. I had His word on it, but I will admit, it was a struggle at times to stay focused on what He said when I saw no evidence that there was money coming in. I had to constantly remind myself of what He said even though there were days that my mind was screaming out for answers.

So, I had a lot on my mind that morning as I woke up. I was praying for some answers and direction, knowing when I went back home, I would have to make some important decisions about all of this and I needed a plan of action. As I was praying that morning, suddenly, the Lord spoke to me and said, "Read Hebrews 11:32-33." I thought, *Well, I think I know that bit of Scripture,* but in obedience, I opened my Bible and read those two verses.

> *And what more shall I say? I do not have time to tell about Gideon, Barak, Samson and Jephthah, about David and Samuel and the prophets, who through faith conquered kingdoms, administered justice, and gained what was promised.*
>
> —Hebrews 11:32-33a

As I was looking at the Scripture, suddenly, I saw it. You see, the eleventh chapter of Hebrews is a hall of fame listing people who had done mighty deeds through God's power. As the writer of Hebrews gets toward the end of the chapter, he says, "Hey, I do not have time to continue and tell you all about these other people that have great stories. But let me tell you how they did it" (my paraphrase). This is what caught my attention, this last sentence, verse 33.

> *Who through faith conquered kingdoms, administered justice, and gained what was promised.*

Here was a very concise and simple formula on how to receive the promises of God. As I stared at it, I realized that God was answering my prayer. He was showing me what to do, how to gain what was promised. So, let's take a look at this sentence and find out exactly what He was saying to me.

The first thing the writer of Hebrews mentions is "through

faith." I think everyone reading this book probably thinks, *Okay, I have faith, not a problem.* Yes, I thought I knew what faith was also—but when things got tough, I found out that I had no clue what faith really was, how to get faith, and why it is required before God can move in the earth realm. How important is faith? Well, it was number one on the list there in Hebrews 11:33, so if you want to gain what was promised, I think you had better make sure you know what faith is and how to know if you are in faith.

Because this is such a vital topic, I have put a special appendix in the back of this book for your review. If you have never read one of my books that covers the topic of faith, then I am going to ask you to go to that appendix and learn what faith is, how to get it, how to know if you are in faith, and if not, what to do about it. Now before you sign off here, thinking you know what faith is and that you are in faith, I am telling you that God had to show me the answers to these questions because, like you, I thought I already knew all about faith. So, please consider reading that appendix even if it is only a review for you.

...IF YOU WANT TO GAIN WHAT WAS PROMISED, I THINK YOU HAD BETTER MAKE SURE YOU KNOW WHAT FAITH IS AND HOW TO KNOW IF YOU ARE IN FAITH.

As a quick review for you, faith is our heart being fully persuaded and in agreement with what heaven says. That agreement, which is called faith, gives heaven legal jurisdiction to move through us, the ones in faith, here in the earth realm. Through faith, we can exercise heaven's jurisdiction and authority and come against Satan's kingdom, capture territory, and bring it under the jurisdiction of God's Kingdom. I understood a lot about faith when God told me to read Hebrews 11:32-33. But it was the middle part of that sentence, that so caught my attention, that He wanted me to see.

> *Who through faith conquered kingdoms, **administered justice**, and gained what was promised.*
>
> —Hebrews 11:33a

As I sat there that morning in 2009, staring at that Scripture, I finally saw what God was trying to tell me. Let me give you my simple interpretation of what God was trying to get to me. I'll explain it through the following analogy. Let's assume that you bought a nice 20-acre piece of ground. You had great hopes of harvesting a good crop on that ground. However, the ground had been left dormant for many years and was covered in weeds. So, the first thing you had to do was to attack those weeds; they had to go. You mowed them down and plowed them under. In keeping with the language of our Scripture in Hebrews chapter 11, let's agree that you conquered the weeds. Yay! That was a great victory and a lot of work. But you also knew you were not finished.

You understood that if you did not plant something else on the land, even though you owned the land, it was basically worthless to you. So, using the terms in our Scripture, if you did not administer the correct seed to that soil, you were never going to gain the promise of a crop. You would be sitting there waiting and waiting for a crop that would never come.

So, let me say it this way. Once you conquer it, you must occupy it. To occupy it, you must administrate what you want there. If you do not administrate what you want there, you just have a field with no weeds and no crop, and you will never realize the promise of that crop you so need. Write this down as it is a very important concept.

You will never occupy what you do not administrate!

Let me give you another example of what I am talking about. When God brought the people of Israel out of Egypt, He did so with a powerful hand. But Pharaoh changed his mind and came after them, and he thought he had them pinned in against the sea. But in reality, we should realize it was God that had them pinned in against the sea. You see, it was God that led them to that exact spot where they would have the sea in front and mountains on the right and left. It was God who knew that Pharaoh was already on his way to recapture them when He told Moses where he should lead them.

As Pharaoh came upon them camped there, the people of Israel realized their situation and found themselves in a very bad place with no escape. But God had a plan, a plan that would end Egypt's claim on them forever. And you know how the story goes: The Red Sea parted, and they crossed over on dry land! But when Pharaoh and his army started to cross, the sea suddenly closed back together over them, and all were drowned. This was a great deliverance. It wasn't that Pharaoh was forced to back off and find another way to get to the nation of Israel. No, they were completely eliminated. But no matter how great that deliverance was, it was really a very small part of their total story. You see, that deliverance only made way for the greater story, their destiny, a place that they were created for and called to occupy.

So, let's understand this very important principle. They were delivered from Egypt to go somewhere, the place of their destiny. Pharaoh was simply a hindrance blocking their future. And it is the same with you. Your problem is simply a hindrance to your future. Although deliverance is part of your story as well, it is where you are going and what you are called to occupy that is your real story! Now, the church loves to celebrate God's deliverance but most of the time fails to realize that deliverance simply frees us to pursue our place of occupation.

We see that the mighty deliverance of Israel from Egypt's hand was only the beginning, not the end. Although free from Pharaoh's bondage, they still had a long way to go before they could actually occupy and enjoy the promise. Years passed, a new generation rose up, and they eventually crossed the wilderness until they came to the Jordan River. On the other side of that river was the Promised Land they had all heard about their entire lives. This is what they had all been dreaming of since Moses led their parents out of Egypt. Remember, the generation that came out of Egypt with Moses died in the wilderness because of their rebellion, except Joshua and Caleb, who believed God.

At this point in the story, Moses has died and Joshua is now leading the next generation into that great Promised Land. As they approached the Jordan River, they saw that it was at flood stage and was then a rushing mighty river unsuitable and dangerous for crossing. But again, just as God told Moses to cross the Red Sea when it seemed to block their path, God told Joshua to move forward and cross the river but to send the priests across first. The nation lined up to cross with the priests out front as God had instructed, and the moment their toes touched the water, the water stopped flowing.

Like the Red Sea crossing they had heard about all their lives, they walked across a dry riverbed. But unlike their parents, who were being delivered from Pharaoh, this water crossing was not a deliverance. Instead, it was a God directed charge toward their future. Yes, the river was an obstacle, just as the Red Sea had been an obstacle to their fathers coming out of Egypt. But in this case, it would serve as a testimony of God's power and ability to take them into the promise as they stood before those walled cities and giants. It would always remind them God would make a way when there seemed to be no way, that He would be with them, and that He would fulfill His promise to them.

Again, no matter how great that river crossing was, they were still not there yet. They still had to administer justice in that place before they could actually "gain" what was promised. Let me explain one more thing. Justice is a legal term meaning administration of law. They would have to enforce God's instructions, His law, in this situation before they could occupy that land and enjoy the promise. Let me point out that even though God got them that far with amazing demonstrations of His power, they still were not occupying anything. They would still have to administer or apply and enforce what God said, which means they would have to take and occupy that land.

You see, their parents made the mistake that so many Christians make. They saw the power of God; they heard the promises regarding the great land that they were heading toward. But they thought that seeing their deliverance was all there was to it. God would do the rest, and they would just step in there, grab their iced teas, and relax. No, they did not realize that they had to administrate justice to gain what was promised. When they realized that they were going to have to get involved and actually face those walled cities and giants, their hearts melted in fear.

This was what God was trying to show me as well. "Gary, you will need to get in there and deal with this situation. You will need to administrate what I want done here." You may ask, "Were you afraid?" Yes, I had to battle fear. My TV broadcast is called *Fixing the Money Thing*, and I owed my friend one million dollars—which I knew was needed not only to pay his staff but also all the vendors who had their own families to take care of—and I had no idea where that one million dollars was going to come from.

On my way home from that meeting, as I was walking through the airport, God spoke to me again. I heard Him clearly say, "Raise up your staff!" I knew He was referring to what Moses did at the Red Sea when he raised his staff and the water parted. I also knew that the staff represented the authority that Moses had as the ordained leader of the nation. I knew then that God was telling me to stand in my authority. I was the head of this ministry. I would have to administrate God's authority and wisdom in this situation if I was ever going to get out of it. I had the promise of that new campus, but until I took charge and administered justice, I would not have the benefit of occupation. Someone was going to have to get in there and figure out a solution—with God's help—to this financial chaos. And that someone was me, the head of the ministry!

Regarding the builder's million dollars, God gave Drenda a plan. We knew that there were no banks lending money in our town during that financial crisis. I even went to my own bank and asked for a loan of $100,000 against my home, which was paid for, just to help get some funds as I knew many people were depending on our payment. My home was worth many hundreds more than what I was asking for. I had perfect credit and great cash flow, but they called me and said they turned me down. I could not believe it, but that is how things were in that hour.

God told Drenda that we should go to our builder's bank and

ask them to loan our church the entire one million dollars. We had never been to this bank or even heard of it, but that is what we did. You see, we figured that if our builder did not get the one million dollars he needed, he may have to file for bankruptcy. He had a business line of credit that was maxed out, and on top of that, he still owed thousands to various vendors. We figured that his bank was already on the hook for most of that money, and we wanted them to transfer that debt to us. If they approved a loan to us, then we would pay our builder, and he would have the funds to pay the bank, his vendors, and staff. The liability would then be transferred to us, and our builder would be free. But remember, this bank knew nothing about us.

So, we put together a presentation of who we were, our history, our forecast of growth, and reasons why they could trust us to pay them back the one million dollars. As I said, we had never been to this bank before and had never met the loan officer. But we made our presentation that day and explained why we thought it was in their best interest to give us the one million dollars. When we were finished making our case, he said, "I have authority to write a check up to $500,000 with no underwriting," and he pulled out a check and wrote it to our church right there on the spot. He then said, "I will get you the other $500,000 next week after I process your request." True story: Without underwriting, without an application filled out, he wrote us a $500,000 check on the spot. Drenda and I sat there in shock as he handed us the check. But please listen to me: That would never have happened if we had not administered that process. Secondly, we needed to be the ones that met the banker. Why? Because we carried the staff, the authority, and anointing of the ministry since we were the heads of the ministry. I could not have sent one of my staff to do that. I am sure they would not have walked out with that check if I had done that. I had to raise up my staff, my authority, with a plan from God to get that done.

Let me continue. How did that $300,000 show up to launch TV? Well, that is a long story in itself, but I will make it quick. Someone in Atlanta got a copy of a small booklet that I had written several years earlier about getting out of debt. We were not on TV yet, not on radio, and had no office or associates in Atlanta at that time. One of my employees from our Ohio office was traveling through the Atlanta airport and had taken my book to read on the plane. As he was waiting in the airport, a man there saw the book in his hands and asked about it. My employee, who was finished reading it, said he could have it.

I HAD TO RAISE UP MY STAFF, MY AUTHORITY, WITH A PLAN FROM GOD TO GET THAT DONE.

This man read the book and was so impressed with it that he called me and said he loved it. He was so impressed with the book that he arranged for me to be on a national television broadcast to talk about it. The producers of the show wanted to offer my material to their audience during the show and asked us if we could produce the product needed, and, of course, we said yes. Amazingly, that show sold so much product that the profit from that one TV appearance paid for a third of the entire cost to start our TV broadcast.

Secondly, I had a man in my church walk up to me after a Sunday morning service and hand me $120,000 toward TV. That was certainly shocking. This man had come to our church totally broke and about to be evicted from his apartment only a couple of years earlier. But as he heard my teaching on the Kingdom, his life began to change. He created several businesses that caused him to really prosper.

Again, you can see the process in this story. I did not just walk out to the mailbox and a check was there to cover everything. I had to go through the process of administrating the details and processes for that TV broadcast, which enabled me to catch those funds. I had to fly there and then do the actual taping. I had my part to play in this story.

The point God was trying to help me see that morning in prayer in regard to Hebrews 11:33 was faith is needed, but it is not all that is needed. We have our parts to play in obtaining the promises.

God can bring the fish, but we have to catch them!

So, let's break this down a bit. Occupation simply means exercising and maintaining your legal dominion over something that you have captured, something that is under your legal jurisdiction. Captured does not necessarily mean something that you have captured through conflict or force, although it could mean that. For instance, just paying for a piece of land captures that land and brings it into your legal jurisdiction. But again, if you do not administrate your will over that land, it will remain dormant and useless. So, what is administration? According to the dictionary, it is the act or process of administering or managing something toward a desired result.

Our text in Hebrews 11 is telling us that we need to administer justice if we want to enjoy the promises of God. This simply means that we have to enforce what God wants in a situation, what His Word, His law says. In regard to our own piece of land, it would mean that we enforce what we want to see happen on that land.

To apply this principle to your business or life, it would mean to administrate the process, which would bring about the desired result you are expecting from something you have under your legal jurisdiction.

This is where people usually miss it. They do not realize that they have a part to play in occupying the promise. And remember, you can never occupy what you do not administrate. Most people simply lean to faith and hope that God will do all the work. But that is not how it works.

Drenda and I have a great house with over 7,000 square feet of space on over 55 acres that we built about 25 years ago. At the time, we were just coming out of debt and learning about the Kingdom, so we were going to do a lot of the work ourselves. We hired a contractor to frame our home and dry it in, and we were going to either do or general contract the rest. And let me say we knew nothing about building a house, and I mean nothing. So, we bought a book on how to build your own house, and away we went. Were we naïve or what? Anyway, that is what we did. I did all the electric in the house, and yet at the time, I had no idea what 12:2 wire was. I knew nothing about electricity. We had a friend that helped with plumbing. We did the tile floors (Drenda did those), we dug trenches, installed all the fixtures, painted the whole house, and more.

...YOU CAN NEVER OCCUPY WHAT YOU DO NOT ADMINISTRATE.

One night, I was exhausted. At the time, we were pastoring our church, out on sales calls every evening for my business, staying up late to work on the house every night, and I was worn out. One day, I started to complain to the Lord about it, and He said, "Well, how did you expect this house to get here?" Yep, I guess I really was asking for that one. But this house is here and has been paid for because of how we built it. We saved a ton of money. On top of that, all our children helped, and it is a very special place to all of us.

God will do His part, but we must do our parts to enjoy His promises.

God told me that administration is a major key to acceleration! Yes, it is the boring details of occupation, but it has to be done. I own a home, and it takes a lot of administration to enjoy it. Taxes, maintenance, and repairs all must be done for the home to function.

So why is administration so important to your acceleration? Let me use an example to explain why. Have you ever driven a car or a maybe a go-cart with a governor on the engine? No matter how much you push the accelerator down, it goes no faster. You see, the carburetor was designed to administrate only a certain flow of fuel to the engine, and no matter how much you want it to go faster, it makes no difference. **Until you change the administration of fuel, you are limited.**

And this is where so many people are, wanting to go faster, but everything is clogged up with administration issues.

To prove my point, let me ask you a question: "Why did Pharaoh put Joseph in charge of the nation of Egypt?" I know what most people will say: "It was because Joseph was able to interpret Pharaoh's dream." But they are wrong. Let me show you.

"It is just as I said to Pharaoh: God has shown Pharaoh what

he is about to do. Seven years of great abundance are coming throughout the land of Egypt, but seven years of famine will follow them. Then all the abundance in Egypt will be forgotten, and the famine will ravage the land. The abundance in the land will not be remembered, because the famine that follows it will be so severe. The reason the dream was given to Pharaoh in two forms is that the matter has been firmly decided by God, and God will do it soon.

And now let Pharaoh look for a discerning and wise man and put him in charge of the land of Egypt. Let Pharaoh appoint commissioners over the land to take a fifth of the harvest of Egypt during the seven years of abundance. They should collect all the food of these good years that are coming and store up the grain under the authority of Pharaoh, to be kept in the cities for food. This food should be held in reserve for the country, to be used during the seven years of famine that will come upon Egypt, so that the country may not be ruined by the famine."

The plan *seemed good to Pharaoh and to all his officials.*

—Genesis 41:28-37

No, it wasn't because Joseph was able to interpret Pharaoh's dream. That gave Joseph the credibility and the platform to speak to Pharaoh from, but it was his detailed administration plan that caught Pharaoh's attention and landed him the job. Let me state a fact here:

Administration saved Egypt! And administration will save you as well.

CHAPTER 3

HOW BIG IS YOUR POTENTIAL?

The day in 2009 that God showed me Hebrews 11:32-33 and spoke to me about how important administration was, He also told me to go to Isaiah 54. There, He showed me a story of acceleration that I needed to understand along with administration. Well, actually, administration was a major part of what He was showing me in Isaiah 54 that day, but there were more details He wanted me to see. At that time, I identified four things that must be done to increase and take more territory. Administration was one of the four. I called these four steps He showed me the four laws for acceleration. I taught these four laws several times over the years, and they are included in this book as four of the nine laws that I learned over time.

I had turned 60 in 2015, and on my birthday, the Lord spoke to me in a dream about the next 10 years of my life. He reminded me of the directive He gave me while in Albania in 2006 where He called me to go to the nations to teach them His covenant of financial blessing. He told me that I would get more done between my 60th and my 70th birthday than I had accomplished in all of my previous ministry years combined. Wow! I remember thinking that was awesome. Of course, I was already committed and staying busy to be faithful to that mission, but that sure was encouraging.

Drenda and I had seen God do some pretty amazing things up to that point in our lives. We had traveled the world preaching and teaching. We had gone on daily TV, which was airing in every time zone in the world. Our church had grown to thousands, and we had seen countless lives changed. We had seen people who the doctors said had four hours to live healed and return to normal life. We had seen people who were pronounced dead at the hospital come to life and who are alive and well today. We had seen tumors just disappear and had seen the paralyzed get up and go back to work the next day. Of course, the most exciting thing was to see thousands upon thousands discover just how awesome the Kingdom of God is, give their hearts to God, and then to see their lives completely transformed. It was an incredible privilege. So, I was excited when He said the next 10 years were going to be even greater than what we had already seen!

In October of 2016, however, something unusual happened. The Lord spoke to me again about administration and the four laws He had previously shown me.

One morning, an angel came into my bedroom and said only four words, "You have a mission." I did not actually see the angel, but I heard him speak. When I asked the Holy Spirit if that was His voice I had heard, He said, "No, it was your angel." Okay, that was cool, but at the time, I was a little confused as I already knew I had a mission, and I had been really busy working on it. So, I began to think about what the angel had said and why he said it. I thought back to when the angel had spoken and tried to pick up on any details that might give me a clue. I remembered there seemed to be an urgency and an authority behind his voice. I sensed he was saying that the assignment that I received from God in Albania was extremely important and that time was short. I guess I could paraphrase his words to mean stay focused and determined and get this done.

After that day, I began to pray about how to go faster and what I should do to make sure I accomplished my mission. It was a couple of months after the angel appeared that I had the dream about this book, as I mentioned in the last chapter. In this dream, I saw this book, I saw the title, and I saw the chapter titles. In the dream, I felt the Lord say that these were nine laws for acceleration that I would need to learn and master if I was going to finish my race with everything accomplished that He had put into my heart. I am not saying that these nine laws are the only laws that govern acceleration, but He told me that these were the ones I needed to master and also to put in this book.

In the dream, He called these nine areas that I would have to learn "the nine laws for acceleration."

I recognized the first four laws as He had already taught me those, and I had been teaching them for years. And indeed, these four laws, according to the chapters in the book that I saw, were to be the first four laws that I was to discuss in the book. After receiving this dream, I began to study and make notes on the other five laws that He showed me. In that study, I saw that there were indeed many things that I had to work on in my personal and ministry life, things that needed some tweaking.

After having that dream, I was so excited to write the book. I thought after such a dramatic and clear dream, I should get started as soon as possible, but I knew that I was not ready yet as there was more to learn before I could. Now, six years after having the dream, I am writing the book, and I am so excited about seeing that dream being fulfilled. But before I get into the actual nine laws for acceleration, I need to lay some groundwork and take you to Isaiah 54, which is the passage where God revealed the first four laws for acceleration.

> *"Sing, barren woman, you who never bore a child; burst into song, shout for joy, you who were never in labor; because more are the children of the desolate woman than of her who has a husband," says the Lord.*
>
> *"Enlarge the place of your tent, stretch your tent curtains wide, do not hold back; lengthen your cords, strengthen your stakes. For you will spread out to the right and to the left; your descendants will dispossess nations and settle in their desolate cities."*
>
> —Isaiah 54:1-3

Here we see a prophecy about a woman who is barren and does not have a husband yet is having more children than a woman who has a husband, all without going into labor. I think that should catch your attention. Your first thought should be, *How could that happen?* I think we can begin to understand the answer to that question by looking at chapter 53. Chapter 53 is a prophecy about Jesus, what He came to do, and how He paid the price of sin for all of us.

Let me show you just a bit of chapter 53, and see if you agree.

> *Surely he took up our pain and bore our suffering, yet we considered him punished by God, stricken by him, and afflicted. But he was pierced for our transgressions, he was crushed for our iniquities; the punishment that brought us peace was on him, and by his wounds we are healed.*

We all, like sheep, have gone astray, each of us has turned to our own way; and the Lord has laid on him the iniquity of us all.

—Isaiah 53:4-6

And the last sentence of that chapter, verse 12, says:

For he bore the sin of many, and made intercession for the transgressors.

I think you will agree that chapter 53 is definitely talking about Jesus. So, with that in mind, let's go straight into chapter 54, verse 1.

Sing, barren woman, you who never bore a child; burst into song, shout for joy, you who were never in labor; because more are the children of the desolate woman than of her who has a husband.

Now, we can ask again, "How could a woman have a baby without going into labor?" And now, you have the answer. Obviously, chapter 54 is talking about the new birth, children that cannot be numbered, born of the Spirit and not of the flesh. Isaiah is talking about you and me and the church. But it speaks of more than just the new birth; it speaks of a completely new covenant. Paul interprets Isaiah 54 for us in Galatians 4:21-31.

Tell me, you who want to be under the law, are you not aware of what the law says? For it is written that Abraham had two sons, one by the slave woman and the other by the free woman. His son by the slave woman was born according to the flesh, but his son by the free woman was born as the result of a divine promise.

These things are being taken figuratively: The women represent two covenants. One covenant is from Mount Sinai and bears children who are to be slaves: This is Hagar. Now Hagar stands for Mount Sinai in Arabia and corresponds to the present city of Jerusalem, because she is in slavery with her children. But the Jerusalem that is above is free, and she is our mother.

—Galatians 4:21-26

Paul interprets the meaning of the two women here in verse 24 as representing two covenants. One woman is in slavery; that represents the old covenant and the law. The second woman represents the new covenant that is not tied to the law but is a new covenant that is based on what Jesus did for us, which is gained by faith. But there is something you may want to pay close attention to that is really huge here! Take a close look at verse 30.

But what does Scripture say? "Get rid of the slave woman and her son, for the slave woman's son will never ***share in the inheritance*** *with the free woman's son."*

—Galatians 4:30

Have you ever received an inheritance? Well, you are not alone. Credit.com surveyed the database and found that 73% of people who died between October and December of 2016 had outstanding debt. The average bill they left on the table was

$61,554.[13] But that is not the type of inheritance you have. No, the inheritance I am talking about is better than anything you have ever heard of.

Paul says you have an inheritance, but he is very clear that you will never be able to receive it by trying to earn it, by trying to be good enough for God on your own. It comes with your adoption into the family of God through Jesus Christ, called being born again. When you are born again, you become part of the family of God, a son or daughter of the house. Remember, you do not have to work for an inheritance; it is given to you, like the woman who had so many children without labor. She simply had to receive them. As I talk about this incredible inheritance, I want you to focus on that statement: She simply had to receive them. She was barren, which was a disgrace in that day. But then, she had countless children, all without her having to labor over their delivery. She simply received them, and that is speaking of the covenant that you now stand in. All of it is available to you now.

REMEMBER, YOU DO NOT HAVE TO WORK FOR AN INHERITANCE; IT IS GIVEN TO YOU...

Your potential has been radically changed!

It is no longer tied to who you are or your ability but is now determined by God, the One giving the inheritance. Sound amazing? Well then, let's take a closer look at your inheritance. Oh? You say you have not received a certified letter stating you have an inheritance. Well, I think you have!

You may have heard people using the term last will and testament when someone dies. What they are talking about is the will that the dead person has written that describes how their

13. Bill Fay, "What Happens When People Die with Debt: Who Pays?" www.debt.org, May 20, 2021

estate will be distributed to their heirs after their death. The word testament means a formal, written directive providing for the disposition of one's property after death, a will.[14]

Part of the Bible we read is called the New Testament, which means it is a formal written directive from God describing what He has given to us. So yes, you have been given a notice of your inheritance. But have you read it? If you received a certified letter stating you have been listed as an heir by your great-uncle, would you open it? Of course you would.

So why do so many people not open the notice of their inheritance, the Bible? Because, first of all, they have never heard of this inheritance. Secondly, all they have heard of is that God is a hard taskmaster. They see God as a God that is mad at them with a full list of dos and don'ts. They know that they have never lived up to that list, so why would they want to read what that God would say to them? They also see God as being unfair and unjust, so they do not even pretend to trust Him and His Word.

For instance, I read a headline about a seven-year-old that died on the operating table during a tonsillectomy. A common and usually very safe operation, her heart just stopped during the operation, an extremely grievous outcome. I think all of our hearts sighed a bit just hearing that it happened. However, as terrible as her death was, there was another tragic part of the story that could affect this family for the rest of their lives. Let me quote what the father said to a reporter (and I am quoting here):

> "You don't understand why these things happen but we know it was God's plan. And that's the only thing that can get us through, because we know it was God."[15]

---

14. www.dictionary.com

15. *New York Post*, February 26, 2020

Let me also quote Green Bay Packers' quarterback, Aaron Rodgers, whose story appeared in *People* magazine on January 22nd, 2020.

> "Rodgers explained that he questioned religion as a kid and has since related to a 'different type of spirituality' as he's gotten older. 'Most people that I knew, church was just … you just had to go. I don't know how you can believe in a God who wants to condemn most of the planet to a fiery hell. What type of loving, sensitive, omnipresent, omnipotent being wants to condemn his beautiful creation to a fiery hell at the end of all this?'"

Crazy comments! But if this is what they believe about God, you would have to agree, who could trust or desire to serve a God who wanted to take their seven-year-old daughter? No one! And who wants to serve a God who "wants" to condemn most of the planet to hell? No one! But that is what the majority of Christians believe. You have heard it all your life, "God allowed it," "God did it," "It was God's plan," "It was their time to go," and many more statements like that. In fact, I am going to bet that you probably think the same way. So I am going to be blunt: If you really believe that God is like that, that He would willingly kill a child or give someone cancer, then we need to have a serious talk. Let me say it this way:

YOU WILL NEVER BELIEVE SOMEONE YOU DON'T TRUST and will certainly not have any interest in reading anything about a so-called inheritance from that person!

This is why I spend so much time sharing with people just

how good God is. Not just by telling them but by showing them as well. The reason I am spending time in this chapter discussing your inheritance, your unlimited potential, is that if I don't help you see the potential that you really have, you will aim too low when we start talking about the nine laws for acceleration. If we can get a picture of who we really are and the greatness of our God, who is for us, I think it will help define the objectives that we set our lives toward. The foundation of that, of course, would be that God is good and we can trust His promises to us.

Let me give you an example by sharing a story that I recently heard from a young lady who attends my church. Amy is a mother of two beautiful young boys, and her greatest joy in life is being a mother. This was her dream ever since she had been married. But for the first three years of her marriage, she could not become pregnant. Instead, she was plagued with miscarriages and discouragement. But one day, she heard of something incredible. A friend had been diagnosed with cancer and given only four days to live but was instantly healed by the power of God. This friend introduced her to my teachings on the Kingdom of God.

One day when talking to this man's wife, the wife asked her if she was trying to have a baby. She answered, "Yes, I am." The wife then said to her, "It is God's will that you have a baby, and your victory is coming." At that, Amy broke down in tears, because she had just experienced a miscarriage. The words were comforting, yet she had no idea why this woman would say something like that. She had always been taught that God knows best, and if she did not become pregnant, then God had a better plan. But this woman's words, to be so confident in what God's will was, intrigued her. She wanted to find out more. In her study of the Word, she came across this Scripture.

Which of you fathers, if your son asks for a fish, will give him a snake instead?

—Luke 11:11

All of a sudden, she realized that if she asked God for a baby, He would give her a baby, not a miscarriage or a barren future. She took that Scripture to heart, and she became pregnant with a baby boy within a few months. Her pregnancy was going great; and later in her pregnancy, she went in to find out what the sex of the baby was. As she was leaving the hospital that day, her phone rang. The nurse asked if she could come back in immediately, because the doctor wanted to talk to her as something had shown up that needed urgent attention. Amy turned around and went back. The doctor told her and showed her that her baby had a hole in his heart, as well as several other health issues that were serious. She was told that she needed to see a specialist right away.

Amy made an appointment with the specialist, which ended up being three days later. During those three days, she and her husband prayed and stayed in the Word concerning the baby and were determined not to lose that baby. After the specialist spent several hours taking pictures and examining him, he came to Amy and said that he had never seen this before, but the hole that had shown up just three days earlier was gone, with only a slight trace of it remaining. The baby was perfectly healthy. Amy was thrilled! She is now a mother of two, and she now knows for a fact that God is good! This is a great story and is one of thousands that I have heard over the years.

God is good, and if you know He is good, what kind of inheritance do you think you have?

In Galatians chapter 4, Paul is writing to a Jewish congregation that has come to know Christ. However, they are still battling with the new concept that the law is no longer needed. Paul is teaching them and correcting them concerning that old way of life, which was slavery.

> *What I am saying is that as long as an heir is underage, he is no different from a slave, although* ***he owns the whole estate****. The heir is subject to guardians and trustees until the time set by his father. So also, when we were underage, we were in slavery under the elemental spiritual forces of the world. But when the set time had fully come, God sent his Son, born of a woman, born under the law, to redeem those under the law, that we might receive adoption to* ***sonship****. Because you are his sons, God sent the Spirit of his Son into our hearts, the Spirit who calls out, "Abba, Father." You are no longer a slave, but God's child; and since you are his child,* ***God has made you also an heir.***
>
> —Galatians 4:1-7

Here, Paul is making the point that after coming to Christ, you are now a son or daughter of God and freed from, as he calls it, the guardian and trustee of the law. The law was a fear based form of righteousness that no one could ever achieve. Thus, sacrifices had to be made year after year, but these sacrifices had no power to free the people from sin. Now through Jesus Christ, the Bible says that in Christ, you have become a new creation.

> *Therefore, if any man be in Christ, he is a new creature: old things are passed away; behold, all things are become new.*
>
> —2 Corinthians 5:17 (KJV)

God's very Spirit now dwells in you, and your enslavement to sin has been broken. As a son or daughter of God, you stand blameless before Him, not on the basis of what you do or did not do but on the basis of who you are. You now qualify for the inheritance, as Paul says in Galatians 4:7. But what is the inheritance? What does the fourth verse say?

THE WHOLE ESTATE!

Wow, that is a pretty awesome inheritance, but I guess it depends on whose estate we are talking about. There are some people's estates that I would not have an interest in at all.

So, whose estate is Paul saying you have inherited?

> *For those who are led by the Spirit of God are the children of God. The Spirit you received does not make you slaves, so that you live in fear again; rather, the Spirit you received brought about your adoption to sonship. And by him we cry, "Abba, Father." The Spirit himself testifies with our spirit that we are God's children. Now if we are children, then we are heirs—* ***heirs of God and co-heirs with Christ****, if indeed we share in his sufferings in order that we may also share in his glory.*
>
> —Romans 8:14-17

Paul says we are heirs of God! That means we have inherited all that God owns! Let that sink in for a moment. You have a legal claim on God's entire estate as one of his sons or daughters. Now, hold on. Paul does not leave it there. He goes on to say that we are co-heirs with Christ. A co-heir speaks of a different

YOU HAVE A LEGAL CLAIM ON GOD'S ENTIRE ESTATE AS ONE OF HIS SONS OR DAUGHTERS.

arrangement than most people think of when they think of an inheritance. We usually think of an inheritance as being divided among the heirs. But in this case, the word co-heir means **to participate in common**. This means that all the heirs share in the inheritance equally; they all own it. For instance, if a husband and wife buy a house, they will probably register it as tenants in common, meaning they both own it in common. If one dies, there is no probate. The living spouse already owns it. Probate is the process of legally proving that someone has a legal claim on the estate. When a property is owned in common, both people already own it, so nothing really changes when one of the spouses dies. There is no confusion, no fighting over who owns what, no legal challenges. The remaining spouse already owns the entire house.

Think about what was just said. You are an heir of God and a co-heir with Jesus. Anything that Jesus has, you have as well. So, remember, you have a legal claim on the entire estate! So, stop your begging, your whining, your wailing, and your sad prayers, hoping to get God's attention. Stop it.

You already have a legal claim on the entire estate!

We do not beg as if we are orphans! We sit at the Father's table, and we can boldly say, "Pass the biscuits." In fact, Jesus said that healing is the children's bread in Mark 7:27, so pass the healing. In fact, there are more than 7,000 promises in the Bible, and they are all yes and amen to you. So enjoy it all; it is already yours! I think Paul pretty well sums it up in Philippians 4:6-7.

You do not need to be anxious about anything!

> *Do not be anxious about anything, but in every situation, by prayer and petition, with thanksgiving, present your requests to God. And the peace of God, which transcends all*

> *understanding, will guard your hearts and your minds in Christ Jesus.*
>
> —Philippians 4:6-7

Do not be anxious! Why? Because you do not need to be anxious if you have access to the answer. Paul says, "*But in every situation....*" You have the answer. I think that would include any problem or need you may encounter. He then tells us how to handle our needs or when we need help with any situation. "*In every situation, by prayer and petition, with thanksgiving, present your requests to God.*" I think most people get the prayer part, well kind of. I will have to talk more about that in a minute, but I think most people understand that prayer is simply talking to God.

"IN EVERY SITUATION, BY PRAYER AND PETITION, WITH THANKSGIVING, PRESENT YOUR REQUESTS TO GOD."

It is the next part that I think most Christians have a problem with, and most have no idea what Paul is talking about. I am talking about that word petition. The definition of petition is a formal, written document requesting a right or benefit from a person or group in authority or a formal written application seeking a court's intervention and action on a matter.[16] Requesting a right or benefit? That sounds like a petition is a very specific request based on a legal standing or relationship. Can you imagine petitioning a court to hear your case, and the judge asks you why you are there? You respond, "Well, I just need some things." "Okay," the judge says, "what do you need, and why do you think this court should hear

16. *The American Heritage Dictionary of the English Language*

your request?" You answer, "I just need some things; that's all." Are you kidding? You have no legal standing in that court if you cannot provide proof of your legal right to be there and exactly why you are there. The judge would just kick you out; that would be a joke.

But, of course, you do have proper legal standing in heaven's court. Why? Because as a citizen of that great Kingdom, you already have a legal claim to it. But let's go back to that word petition. We understand that we need to pray, but what is our petition? In light of the definition of the word petition we previously mentioned, how would you answer? What would your formal, written request look like? How would you write a formal application seeking a court's intervention and action on a matter? I think you would agree it would be with great detail.

Well, I can tell you how most people pray—with a very vague and "if it be your will" request. They are not sure of their legal standing, and they are not sure what is legally theirs. If a person does not understand those two things when they go to prayer, then the only thing left to do is to beg. Let me help you out: **Stop it**. You would never go to court without a very detailed request, along with the legal paperwork to prove that your request is a legal and just request of the court.

So many Christians have no idea what their legal standing is, have no idea how to petition heaven's court on the basis of their legal standing, or what is legally theirs in the Kingdom. Many get offended when I talk about and teach these principles. They tell me that it would be disrespectful to demand anything from God. We are not demanding anything from God. We are simply saying, "Pass the biscuits." You ALREADY own the biscuits; God has already given them to you. He is offended when we do not receive what He has given us.

If I had a large deposit in my bank, went in to make a withdrawal, and the teller told me that I could not have my money, what would I do? "Oh, I am sorry that I bothered you. How foolish of me to make such a request from such a prestigious bank." Is that what I would do? NO! I would demand my money; it was already mine. When I go to the bank, I make a very detailed withdrawal. I do not say, "Hey, you guys know what is best. Just give me some money; you decide."

A petition is very detailed, but it cannot be detailed if you do not know what you have.

Let me give you an example of what a specific request looks like. Years ago, when we were just learning how the Kingdom operated, I wanted a motorcycle. We were still living in the old farmhouse at the time, and we did not have a garage. So, I sowed a seed for a new Honda ST 1100 that I saw one day and thought looked like a great bike to own. However, when I sowed my seed for that bike, I wrote on my check that I did not want it to show up until I had a nice garage to put it in. Why? Because I did not want to keep it outside in the weather. My pastor at the time loved to ride motorcycles. Every year, I would write him a check for $300 and would write on the check: Gas money for your riding and seed for my ST 1100. I also bought three used motorcycles for other pastors and friends, all along saying that was seed for my ST 1100.

Well, after we built our house, we did have a nice garage. One day, a couple showed up at my house with a brand-new ST 1300 and gave it to me for my birthday. Honda had just redesigned the 1100 with a newer, more powerful engine—the Honda ST 1300. It was just as I dreamed it would be. It was an awesome bike that I rode for 14 years. I have since replaced it with a Harley Ultra Limited that I use for touring. But I wanted you to know how specific my petition was, and that was exactly what showed up. And this is always what will show up.

I can tell you so many stories of how the Kingdom is so specific and how your petition needs to also be specific. A few years ago, we had our church rent a couple of Escalades for a conference we were hosting. We rented them to drive our guests around, and we wanted to provide a nice vehicle to do so. Now, this was not the first time we had done that. We have always done that. But it was the first time I had driven one of them while we had them on the property for an event. I am not sure why we drove one during this particular event, but we drove it home overnight. And you know what? I loved it. Drenda and I loved how it drove and how it looked.

At the time, we were driving a nice Honda Pilot, but the Escalade was a step above the Pilot for sure. It was the platinum pearl white model and was the shorter version. If you know much about these Escalades, they come in two sizes, the long one and a shorter one. We liked the short one better as it seemed to handle better with a little more agile maneuverability. As I was driving the Escalade with Drenda, she said, "You know, I like this. I think we should get one of these." I agreed, "We should get one just like this one, the short version in pearl white." We both agreed.

Although we did not tell anyone about our conversation, about a month later, as I was walking outside to pick up my paper, my cell phone rang. I recognized the voice on the other end of the line as someone who attended my church. He said hello and then said that he wanted to buy me an Escalade. I was taken aback for a minute but said, "Great!" He then asked me what color I would like, and I told him that we loved the pearl white one. He said, "I will call you back when I get one for you." He did not ask me if I wanted the short one or the long one, however.

A month went by, and I thought maybe he had forgotten about the car, but sure enough, he called and told us to come by, that he had the Escalade ready for us to pick up. As we met him, we saw a beautiful pearl white short version Escalade sitting there. It was perfect in every way, without a scratch, literally perfect. We told him we loved it. He then apologized. He said he was sorry it took so long to get back to us, but although he had tried to find a long version, all he could find was the short one. We laughed and said, "The short one is the one we wanted." We drove that car home and thought we were the richest people on the planet driving that car.

Again, I could fill an entire book with illustrations of just how specific the Kingdom is. So, when Philippians is talking about a petition, it means just what it says. Again, you are not begging; you are making a requisition. It is no different than one of my kids saying, "Hey, Dad, pass the biscuits." My kids do not beg me for the food they eat. They act like they own it, which they do.

I like how the Lord's Prayer teaches us to pray, and I think it shows you another great example of the posture we are to take in prayer. Very simply, it says, "*Give us this day our daily bread.*" Pretty direct, don't you think? In fact, Jesus rebuked the religious folks because they were begging and carrying on with long prayers, just hoping that God would do something for them.

> *And when you pray, do not keep on babbling like pagans, for they think they will be heard because of their many words. Do not be like them, for your Father knows what you need before you ask him.*
>
> *This then is how you should pray:*

> *"Our Father in heaven, hallowed be your name, your kingdom come, your will be done on earth as it is in heaven. Give us today our daily bread."*
>
> —Matthew 6:7-11

I know the prayer went on further than I have quoted here, but I have quoted enough to make my point. They thought they would be heard because of their many words. What does that tell you? They had no idea of their legal standing before heaven, and sadly, it is the same today for so many as well. When Jesus says they think they will be heard because of their many words, the word heard here is not implying that God is not listening. He is listening like a judge who hears a case. God takes the case, and justice will be done. Because they did not understand their legal standing in the courts of heaven, all that was left to do was beg with long prayers, just hoping that God would do something for them. And what did Jesus say about that? **Stop it!** Pray like this.

Remember, the Lord's Prayer is a template teaching us how to pray. Most of the time, people just quote it as if it is a prayer. No, He is showing you how to pray. The prayer postures your legal standing in the first line: "Our Father." He is your Father, meaning you have a legal claim and a right to receive from Him. It then goes on and instructs you how to bring your petition before Him. You are there to make a claim on what heaven says is yours, and now your requisition is going to bring that legal claim into the earth realm from the heavenly realm. When you make your request, it is not begging for mercy, but rather, "Give me this day my daily bread." Notice there is no begging in that statement. It is simple and to the point: Pass the biscuits. You can actually put anything in that line that you need. Again, it is a template on how to pray, and it does not just refer to bread. It simply says:

Give me this day my daily bread.

Your requisition is bringing what is in heaven into the earth realm, which is totally in line with what Jesus taught.

> *Truly I tell you, whatever you bind on earth will be bound in heaven, and* ***whatever you loose*** *on earth will be loosed in heaven.*
>
> —Matthew 18:18

Let me paraphrase what we have just read. Nothing in the heavenly realm is going to show up here on Earth in your life unless you make a legal claim to it! Why? Because it has no legal jurisdiction to do so until you do so.

Several years ago, I had a young lady in my church who was having trouble with the spirit of fear. One day while talking to her, I was trying to locate the root, the door that Satan had used to torment her. She then told me that when she was young, she grew up in a wealthy home and had a beautiful bedroom. Her bed had beautiful pillows, and the bedspread was stunning. "On the bedspread were the most amazing dolls," she said. But although she had her own bedroom, she never slept in it. She had to sleep in the basement so as not to mess up her room. Her mother would kick her out of the house in the mornings and not

NOTHING IN THE HEAVENLY REALM IS GOING TO SHOW UP HERE ON EARTH IN YOUR LIFE UNLESS YOU MAKE A LEGAL CLAIM TO IT!

allow her to come in until evening, and then only after taking her shoes off and making sure there was not one blade of grass on her clothes. So even though this young girl had rich parents and had beautiful things, she could not enjoy them and was forced to live like an orphan. How sad. No wonder this young woman had such a hard time receiving from God and battled fear and depression. But, thank God, through consistent retraining of her mind, she walked out of that prison of fear, and so can you. To walk free from the lies of the religious culture and fully understand who you are and what you have, you will need to reprogram your mind as well.

> *Therefore, I urge you, brothers and sisters, in view of God's mercy, to offer your bodies as a living sacrifice, holy and pleasing to God—this is your true and proper worship. Do not conform to the pattern of this world but be transformed by the renewing of your mind. Then you will be able to test and approve what God's will is—his good, pleasing and perfect will.*
>
> —Romans 12:1-2

Pardon me for a minute, but I need to be really blunt here. You will never be able to receive God's inheritance until you reprogram your religious mind to the truth of who you are in the Kingdom. Paul knew this when he wrote to the church in Ephesus about this very thing.

> *For this reason, ever since I heard about your faith in the Lord Jesus and your love for all God's people, I have not stopped giving thanks for you, remembering you in my prayers. I keep asking that the God of our Lord Jesus Christ, the glorious Father, may give you the Spirit of wisdom and revelation, so*

> *that you may know him better. I pray that the eyes of your heart may be enlightened in order that you may know the hope to which he has called you, the riches of his glorious inheritance in his holy people, and his incomparably great power for us who believe. That power is the same as the mighty strength he exerted when he raised Christ from the dead and seated him at his right hand in the heavenly realms, far above all rule and authority, power and dominion, and every name that is invoked, not only in the present age but also in the one to come.*
>
> —Ephesians 1:15-21

Paul says, "*I pray that the eyes of your heart may be enlightened in order that you may know the hope to which he has called you, the riches of his glorious inheritance in his holy people*." The word enlightened means to be illuminated. He is praying that the Holy Spirit will help you see just how great of an inheritance you have in Christ. He calls it a glorious inheritance! Our inheritance in Christ is a spiritual inheritance, of course, but also it is a physical inheritance here in the earth realm.

I thought I would just touch on a small part of your inheritance that few Christians understand, the blessing of Abraham. Some people think that because we have a New Testament that all the benefits of the Old Testament have been nullified—not true.

> *Christ redeemed us from the curse of the law by becoming a curse for us, for it is written: "Cursed is everyone who is hung on a pole." He redeemed us in order that* ***the blessing given to Abraham might come to the Gentiles through Christ Jesus****, so that by faith we might receive the promise of the Spirit.*
>
> —Galatians 3:13-14

So exactly what is the blessing of Abraham? I think you need to know since you have it.

Going back in time, at the beginning when the earth was created, God placed Adam and Eve over the earth to rule it on behalf of His Kingdom. Satan, who had already been cast down to the earth, lusted after the authority that man had been given. Satan then put a plan in place to deceive Adam and Eve into following him. By lying to them about God's character and promising them a better life, Adam and Eve willingly chose to follow Satan and forsake God. Because God had given them absolute authority over the earth, God could not stop them (Hebrews 2:7-8). The result? We find that in Genesis 3:17b-19.

> *Cursed is the ground <u>because of you</u>; through painful toil you will eat food from it all the days of your life. It will produce thorns and thistles for you, and you will eat the plants of the field. By the sweat of your brow you will eat your food until you return to the ground, since from it you were taken; for dust you are and to dust you will return.*

The earth became cursed, which simply means the earth lost the blessing of God. And please notice that God blamed Adam for this. He did not curse the earth; Adam did. Let me say it this way: Adam literally kicked God out of his life! The earth that was once so luscious and green would now produce thistles and thorns. Adam and Eve, who had so easily eaten from the Garden of God, would now have a life of surviving by their own painful toil and sweat. God lost His influence over mankind as Satan became the god of this world.

> *The god of this age has blinded the minds of unbelievers, so that they cannot see the light of the gospel that displays the glory of Christ, who is the image of God.*
>
> —2 Corinthians 4:4

The worst consequence of Adam's rebellion was that all mankind, his lineage, was then separated from God and under Satan's jurisdiction. In all of Satan's tempting, he left one small detail out. It was that his judgment had already been set and his destiny was a place called hell. Now, man, being a part of Satan's kingdom and under his spiritual jurisdiction, would be taken there as well. This was not God's decision. It was Adam's. Hell was never prepared for mankind, as Matthew 25:41 says.

> *...the eternal fire prepared for the devil and his angels.*
>
> —Matthew 25:41b

Most people think going to heaven or hell is based on what they do, and if they are good enough they will go to heaven. But let me say this clearly:

Going to heaven or hell has nothing to do with how good or bad you are.

When Adam rebelled against God, he took all of mankind to hell with him. I do not want to sound blunt here, but I need to be. Everyone is already going to hell because of Adam, and there is only one way out. The only escape from that judgment is that your name be written in the Lamb's Book of Life, which is in heaven. And the only way that happens is if you believe Jesus is who He said He was and call on His name for your salvation.

> *And everyone who calls on the name of the Lord will be saved.*
>
> —Acts 2:21

Jesus called this being born again; and if you have not called on the name of Jesus, I would encourage you to do that now. You see, Jesus was God's rescue plan to bring His creation back into His Kingdom where He had originally designed man to live. But because each man, woman, and child has a free will and has legal jurisdiction over their own life, God cannot make anyone receive his free gift of life.

> *For he has rescued us from the dominion of darkness and brought us into the kingdom of the Son he loves.*
>
> —Colossians 1:13

When Adam and Eve fell, God lost His representation in the earth. He had to find another man who would give Him access into the earth realm, so He could put His rescue plan in place. That man was Abram, who would later be named Abraham. Abraham and Sarah were advanced in years, and Sarah was past the age to conceive a child. Yet God appeared to them and told them that they would indeed have a son. Abraham believed God, and God made a legal agreement, an oath, swearing to Abraham that this would certainly come to pass.

This covenant would once again give God access to bless mankind but only through Abraham and his heirs, as the covenant was made between God and Abraham and his heirs. It was through this covenant and this lineage that Jesus came into the world. To most, the first chapter of the book of Matthew is a very boring list of begats, but it is a very detailed record of Abraham's genealogy all the way to Jesus's birth. This chapter is not as boring as you may assume for it proves that Jesus came through that promise to Abraham. It is written there to bear witness before heaven and Earth, for all to see, and it verifies that Jesus came legally into the earth realm. It is especially important to Satan, the god of this world who would have challenged Jesus's legality, but the evidence is there for all to see.

Okay, now that we know who Abraham was, let's get back to our discussion of the blessing of Abraham and how that affects us here in the New Testament. When God made that covenant with Abraham, He made promises to Abraham. God told Abraham that he would become a great nation and that He would bless all the nations of the earth through him, which, of course, was referring to the fact that Jesus would come through his lineage. God said that He would bless Abraham. These promises that God gave to Abraham are called the blessing of Abraham.

We must remember that Abraham was not born again, because Jesus had not yet come to pay the price of sin, thus Abraham could not go into the presence of God. But Abraham held the promise that through his own seed, the Messiah would come and pay the price of salvation. Until then, God gave Abraham promises which dealt with the earth realm, declaring how He was going to bless him and give him great influence over the earth.

Up until this time, Satan was holding man hostage to a life of slavery and poverty as a result of Adam's sin. But through the promises of Abraham, God could then legally override the earth's curse of Adam's rebellion and bless Abraham. Instead of Abraham being limited to his own painful toil and sweat, God declared that He would make Abraham great and prosper him.

As we read in Galatians, these promises are still true to us today—the blessing of Abraham.

CHAPTER 4

THE BLESSING OF ABRAHAM

As I said in the previous chapter, as a New Testament believer, you have the spiritual inheritance of the new birth but also the blessing of Abraham. Again, the blessing of Abraham is the promises that God made to Abraham describing who he was, his future, and the vast wealth he would someday have. To set the stage for our discussion, let's go back to that verse in Genesis 3:17-19 regarding the fall of man.

> *Cursed is the ground* <u>*because of you;*</u> *through painful toil you will eat food from it all the days of your life.* ***It will produce thorns and thistles for you, and you will eat the plants of the field. By the sweat of your brow you will eat your food*** *until you return to the ground, since from it you were taken; for dust you are and to dust you will return.*
>
> —Genesis 3:17b-19

The earth curse—by painful toil and by the sweat of our brows, we would make our way through life. Basically, your potential under this system would be your own toil. Of course, we all were born under this system of survival and have trained ourselves to evaluate our chance of success through this filter—how much labor will it cost us? But the promises that God gave Abraham in Genesis chapter 12 changed all that.

> *The Lord had said to Abram, "Go from your country, your people and your father's household to the land I will show you. I will make you into a great nation, and I will bless you; I will make your name great, and you will be a blessing. I will bless those who bless you, and whoever curses you I will curse; and all peoples on earth will be blessed through you."*
>
> —Genesis 12:1-3

Did you see the change? God said,

"I will make you!"

Think about that. God said, "I will make you" to Abraham. He would no longer be held captive to a future that he had to create or make happen through his own painful toil and sweat. God was telling him that He was going to make him. In other words, God had a legal door through Abraham's faith to bless him. God had promised Abraham that He would bless him, make his name great, and that he would become a great nation. God also said that through him, all peoples on Earth would be blessed, which was referring to the fact that Jesus would come through his lineage. These promises that God gave to Abraham, as I have said, are called the blessing of Abraham. To be sure that Abraham knew just how great these promises were, God gave him several pictures of what He wanted to do through him.

> *After this, the word of the Lord came to Abram in a vision: "Do not be afraid, Abram. I am your shield, your very great reward."*
>
> *But Abram said, "Sovereign Lord, what can you give me*

since I remain childless and the one who will inherit my estate is Eliezer of Damascus?" And Abram said, "You have given me no children; so a servant in my household will be my heir."

*Then the word of the Lord came to him: "This man will not be your heir, but a son who is your own flesh and blood will be your heir." He took him outside and said, "**Look up at the sky and count the stars**—if indeed you can count them." Then he said to him, "So shall your offspring be."*

*Abram believed the Lord, and he credited it to him as righteousness. He also said to him, "I am the Lord, who brought you out of Ur of the Chaldeans **to give you this land to take possession of it**."*

—Genesis 15:1-7

God uses two pictures here to help Abraham grasp the magnitude of the promises He is giving him. First, He says to "count the stars, if you can. That is how many heirs you will have." Of course, at the time of this conversation, Abraham had no children at all. Secondly, God lays out the boundaries of all the land that Abraham will inherit, which was over 35 million acres! Which would be more than he could ever walk out. To paraphrase how big Abraham's inheritance was, let's just say it was bigger than he could count!

This blessing of the Lord that was on Abraham had an immediate effect. Only one chapter later after receiving God's promise, we see a huge change.

Abram had become very wealthy in livestock and in silver and gold.

—Genesis 13:2

As we can see, he truly escaped the earth curse system of painful labor and sweat.

Now, let's move forward in time to when the Israelites were leaving Egypt for the Promised Land. Before they were to cross over into the land, God wanted them to understand just how great their inheritance would be. So, He tells them this through Moses in Deuteronomy 6:10-12.

> *When the Lord your God brings you into the land he swore to your fathers, to Abraham, Isaac and Jacob, to give you—a land with large, flourishing cities* ***you did not build****, houses filled with all kinds of good things* ***you did not provide****, wells* ***you did not dig****, and vineyards and olive groves* ***you did not plant****—then when you eat and are satisfied, be careful that you do not forget the Lord, who brought you out of Egypt, out of the land of slavery.*
>
> —Deuteronomy 6:10-12

I think you get the point; they were going to inherit all this without labor! Let's remember that as Israel took over these lands, it was judgment on the people who lived there as they were extremely wicked.

> *After the Lord your God has driven them out before you, do not say to yourself, "The Lord has brought me here to take possession of this land because of my righteousness." No, it is on account of the wickedness of these nations that the Lord is going to drive them out before you. It is not because of your righteousness or your integrity that you are going in to take possession of their land; but on account of the wickedness of*

> *these nations, the Lord your God will drive them out before you, to accomplish what he swore to your fathers, to Abraham, Isaac and Jacob. Understand, then, that it is not because of your righteousness that the Lord your God is giving you this good land to possess, for you are a stiff-necked people.*
>
> —Deuteronomy 9:4-6

But the point I am making is in the first sentence of Deuteronomy 6:10, "*When the Lord your God brings you into the land he swore to ... Abraham.*"

God will bring you into the land.

It was not that they had to battle their way in there leaning to their own strength; God was going to take them in Himself.

I will make you!

Probably the best place in the Bible that lays out the blessing of Abraham is Deuteronomy 28. As we read through this, please put your name in here, because these promises are all yours now as it was theirs then.

> *If you fully obey the Lord your God and carefully follow all his commands I give you today, the Lord your God will set you high above all the nations on earth. All these blessings will come on you and accompany you if you obey the Lord your God:*
>
> > *You will be blessed in the city and blessed in the country.*
> >
> > *The fruit of your womb will be blessed, and the crops of your land and the young of your livestock—the calves of your herds and the lambs of your flocks.*
> >
> > *Your basket and your kneading trough will be blessed.*

You will be blessed when you come in and blessed when you go out.

The Lord will grant that the enemies who rise up against you will be defeated before you. They will come at you from one direction but flee from you in seven.

The Lord will send a blessing on your barns and on everything you put your hand to. The Lord your God will bless you in the land he is giving you.

The Lord will establish you as his holy people, as he promised you on oath, if you keep the commands of the Lord your God and walk in obedience to him. Then all the peoples on earth will see that you are called by the name of the Lord, and they will fear you.

The Lord will grant you abundant prosperity—in the fruit of your womb, the young of your livestock and the crops of your ground—in the land he swore to your ancestors to give you.

The Lord will open the heavens, the storehouse of his bounty, to send rain on your land in season and to bless all the work of your hands. You will lend to many nations but will borrow from none.

The Lord will make you the head, not the tail. If you pay attention to the commands of the Lord your God that I give you this day and carefully follow them, you will always be at the top, never at the bottom. Do not turn aside from any of the commands I give you today, to the right or to the left, following other gods and serving them.

—Deuteronomy 28:1-14

Yes, this is you! I hope you can now see why I wanted you to read this. You do not see a survival mentality here at all. Whatever you put your hands to shall prosper!

"*The Lord will establish you as his holy people.*" Established? Most people are not established. An oak tree that is 100 years old is established; no one can move it! But for most people, that concept is foreign. Their lives are full of stress, just trying to stay ahead of the insecurity that surrounds them. They own nothing! Everything is purchased on payments, and if the payments are not made, then the legal owner comes and takes their possessions away. Established means you cannot be moved, in good times or bad times.

God is telling Israel that no one will be able to move them out of their own land, and the emphasis is on the word own. Established means you own it! No debt. You own it. The text goes on and says, "*Then all the peoples on earth will see that you are called by the name of the Lord, and they will fear you. The Lord will grant you abundant prosperity.*" God says that when they are established, people will see that they are called by the name of the Lord. How? God is invisible, so how are the ungodly going to see God? Verse 11 tells us, "*The Lord will grant you abundant prosperity!*" They will see your wealth and will have to acknowledge that God has blessed you. If that is not enough, the text goes on and says, "*You will lend to many nations but will borrow from none. The Lord will make you the head, not the tail.*" You will be so blessed that you will be the lender, not the borrower. You will be the head and not the tail.

YOU WILL BE SO BLESSED THAT YOU WILL BE THE LENDER, NOT THE BORROWER.

No debt! This is part of your inheritance.

Now, I need to ask you something. If what we have just read is true, and it is, and if I have proven to you that as a New Testament believer, you have those same promises, would it change anything about your life? If you received a one-billion dollar inheritance today from a rich uncle, would it change your life tomorrow? I think so.

> *"Sing, barren woman, you who never bore a child; burst into song, shout for joy, you who were never in labor; because more are the children of the desolate woman than of her who has a husband," says the Lord.*
>
> *"Enlarge the place of your tent, stretch your tent curtains wide, do not hold back; lengthen your cords, strengthen your stakes."*
>
> —Isaiah 54:1-2

We have already talked about how a woman could have more children without having labor than a woman who has labor. We now know that Isaiah was talking about the spiritual new birth, being born again by the Spirit of God. And we found out that the two women represent two covenants—the old covenant of slavery, which is the ordinary way, and the new covenant with the born-again experience, which transforms us by the power of the Spirit. The effect of this new covenant is made clear in the example that Isaiah uses. One woman conceives and delivers a baby through the ordinary nine-month gestation way. But the other covenant is not limited by the flesh, is conceived by a promise, and is born by the power of the Spirit. We have the unlimited way verse, not the limited way. We are no longer limited by our own experiences or ability. Remember, God made Abraham. He could not have children, but he did.

Remember my story. I tried for nine years to make my business work out, but it didn't work. With God, it did, and now I am a millionaire. I thought it was not possible to be in the top 10 with one of my vendors due to my schedule. I had been doing about 4 million in production with them for 14 years straight and did not think it was possible to be in the top 10. But I did get in the top 10, and I have received the $100,000 bonus check that the top 10 get now years in a row.

My daughter Amy had a 13-pound tumor in her abdomen, and it seemed there was no way to avoid surgery, but she did. One night as she slept, the tumor disappeared. She lost 13 pounds; 9 inches in her waist; and her back, which was knotted and twisted, was totally recreated.

My daughter-in-law was told she had four months to live as she had a huge tumor in her hip area, but she didn't die. The tumor disappeared one night as she slept as well.

I could go on and on, but you get the picture. Your future is no longer limited. God says He will make you. Because of this huge transformation, Isaiah says you need to prepare for increase. Remember, Abraham was told that his inheritance was more than he could ever count. Guess what? He has declared the same thing to you.

> *Now to him who is able to do immeasurably more than all we ask or imagine, according to his power that is at work within us.*
>
> —Ephesians 3:20

God is able to do more than you can imagine!!!!

After Isaiah declares that this new covenant is going to cause supernatural increase in verse 1 of Isaiah 54, he then explains what we need to do to prepare for this harvest in the following verses. In the next four verses, he lays out four primary things we need to do to receive this increase. These are the first four laws for acceleration!

Let me give you another example of how this works. Last year, 2021, because of Covid, our production was just a little stagnant. I had sown and asked God for 2021 to be the best year I had ever had in business. It was the fall of 2021, and things were not really moving forward and not really falling backwards but just consistent. But, of course, I had not sown for consistent. I had sown for the best year I had ever had.

In the early part of November, I had a dream. In the dream, I saw a picture of my open wallet, and it was full of money. The Lord spoke to me in that dream and said, "I can yet do something big before the year is out." Wow, what a great encouragement.

A couple of weeks later, a guy called and said he wanted to talk about our investments that he had heard so much about. He had heard that over the last 20 years, we had never had a client lose money due to market swings. Seeing how turbulent things were becoming in the United States, he was curious. So, I met with him, explained our investment strategy to him, and he loved it. Well, to make a long story short, he invested a rather large amount of money. Due to having him as a client, along with a few more last-minute "they called me" clients, I had the best year I have ever had in business.

All I can say is that the laws of the Kingdom and the anointing to prosper brought that money in. But let me say that the money did not just show up. I am the one who laid out my petition to receive that money, and it came to pass just as I had sown. Incredible!

CHAPTER 5

THE LAW OF DOMINION

As I said in chapter 4, due to this new covenant, a lot of things are going to change. Let me rephrase that: Everything is going to change! After Isaiah prophesied about this new covenant and our birth into the Kingdom of God, he went on to say how this was going to change how we live. Being born again now gives us access to the entire estate of God as a member of God's own household. Like Abraham, we have now escaped from the earth curse system and literally have changed kingdoms. As I said earlier, verse 2 contains the first four laws for acceleration. These four laws are the laws God showed me when we were in such a financial mess with the Now Center. They are extremely powerful concepts that will help you accelerate your business or whatever you need to see move faster. Let's start with the first of the nine laws for acceleration—**the law of dominion**.

> *Enlarge the place of your tent, stretch your tent curtains wide, do not hold back; lengthen your cords, strengthen your stakes.*
>
> —Isaiah 54:2

Enlarge the place of your tent.

Here is the first instruction that God gives: Enlarge the place of your tent, not the tent itself but the place of the tent. The tent represents your life, and the place would refer to your vision for your life. Instead of surviving on that quarter acre lot mindset, Isaiah said that you are going to need more room, a lot more room, to be able to receive all that is in your inheritance. This law says to enlarge the place where you live, increase your territory, your dominion. Remember, God can only bless what is under your legal jurisdiction.

This will be your choice!

Deuteronomy 28:8 says:

> *The Lord will send a blessing on your barns and on everything you put your hand to. The Lord your God will bless you in the land he is giving you.*

You have the blessing, but again, if something is not under your jurisdiction, then God has no legal jurisdiction over it. So here is the question: Do you want 3 tomato plants that are blessed or 50,000? If you knew that whatever you put under that anointing would prosper, how much would you put there? Oh, the temptation to fall back into our old mindset with that question. Our say no before you even consider saying yes training kicks in here. But you are not alone in this decision. The Bible says that you can ask God for help.

> *If any of you lacks* ***wisdom****, you should ask God, who gives generously to all without finding fault, and it will be given to you.*
>
> —James 1:5

But for most people, they do not even get that far as their no training shuts the door without any consideration that God is trying to get something to them. I know. I have done that, too, many times, and it has cost me thousands.

For instance, I had an experience about a year or so ago that so clearly points out this wrong default setting. I need to be aware of how easily it tries to pop up. Even now after all these years, if I am not careful, it will umpire a decision when it shouldn't.

One day, 2 Corinthians 9:10-11 just kept going through my head, and I just could not shake it. I knew the Lord was trying to teach me something, and I was meditating on the Scripture, allowing the Holy Spirit to speak to me about it. The part of the text that kept rolling through my head was, "*he who supplies seed to the sower and bread for food.*"

> *Now **he who supplies seed to the sower and bread for food** will also supply and increase your store of seed and will enlarge the harvest of your righteousness. You will be enriched in every way so that you can be generous on every occasion, and through us your generosity will result in thanksgiving to God.*
>
> —2 Corinthians 9:10-11

As I continued thinking on this Scripture, the Holy Spirit seemed to zoom in and illuminate, "*and bread for food*"; that portion just kind of jumped out at me. I realized that so many people face fear when they want to give because they do not understand that phrase. Most people think that when they give, they are giving up something, that it is going to cost them. But what God was reminding me of was that not only does He provide the seed to sow, but also He provides the bread for eating, what a person needs personally. Of course, I already knew that, but I felt that He wanted to make sure I told people that, that they understood He gives us both and they do not need to be afraid to give.

HE PROVIDES THE SEED TO SOW, BUT ALSO HE PROVIDES THE BREAD FOR EATING, WHAT A PERSON NEEDS PERSONALLY.

On this particular night, a couple of weeks after we had sown $15,000 to a ministry we supported, I was about to turn the lights off and head to bed when, suddenly, I had a thought to check the stock market on a few stocks I own to see how they were doing. As I pulled up my account, I saw that they had indeed moved up some. As I was about to put my phone down, my eyes were drawn to one particular stock that I did not own. I had seen this stock before, and I had looked at it once, even considered buying it. When I investigated its past performance, I saw that it had been flat for the previous 12 months, so I passed. But for some reason this night, this stock seemed to jump out at me. Strangely, I felt that I should buy some of it, which was totally out of character for me. So, I went ahead and bought $1,500 of this stock and set my phone down.

Drenda and I talked for a little while, and I told her about the stock purchase and pulled it up to show her. As I pulled it up, I sat there shocked as it had gone up over 100 percent in the previous hour. We stayed awake and talked as we watched the numbers slowly keep going up. Over the next three hours, the stock had moved up to being worth over $17,000, where it leveled off. I told Drenda, "That is our $15,000!" I quickly sold the stock and captured the increase, and I knew this was a return of the $15,000 I had sown a couple of weeks earlier. The stock went right back down by morning and has never regained that level now months after that event occurred. That was the weirdest thing I have ever seen. I know that it was the Holy Spirit who illuminated that stock to me, and I told Drenda it was God returning our seed. God gives seed to the sower, and He gives bread for the eating! You know, I don't care how He does it, but He always does it. But it was interesting.

After I sold that stock and had the money back in my account, I thought, *Boy, if I had known it was going to go up like that, I would have put a lot more than $1,500 in*. Well, looking back is always with 20/20 vision. Yes, I could have put $10,000 in, or your mind drifts and thinks, *What if I had put $100,000 in*? Think of the amount of money I would have made on that investment. But I didn't put $100,000 in. I didn't put $10,000 in. I didn't put $5,000 in. I put $1,500 in. You see, my profit was capped. I put in $1,500, and although I sure would have liked more, that was not going to happen because I had only put in $1,500. So, what happened? I had half of it right. I sensed that I should buy some of that stock, but I did not ask the Lord how much I should buy. I allowed my normal default setting in my brain to make that decision without me even thinking about it. Yes, I got the $15,000 back, my original seed, but I did not get the second half of that promise.

> *Now he who supplies seed to the sower and bread for food will also supply* ***and increase your store of seed and will enlarge the harvest of your righteousness****.*
>
> —2 Corinthians 9:10

I did not get the increase and the enlarged harvest that should have been mine. God had a lot more in store for me that night, not just getting my seed back, although that was great. But I did not ask God how much to put in and thus missed the increase that would have been mine if I would have asked. Why didn't I ask God? I was busy and did not think much of it until after it went up like a rocket. It is easy to let the old default setting speak, but we can reset our default setting to stop and consider and to not be so hasty in our own understanding. Ask God for wisdom in situations like that, and you will see some big results.

Here is what the Lord spoke to me one day: "Make no small plans!"

THERE IS MORE!

So many people miss so many opportunities that God sets in front of them. They plant the three tomato plants, and when they turn out perfect, they say, "Well, I should have sown more." And as I showed you, it is easy to do.

Let's look at some verses in Genesis concerning Abraham.

> *The Lord said to Abram after Lot had parted from him, "Look around from where you are, to the north and south, to the east and west. All the land that you see I will give to you and your offspring forever. I will make your offspring like the dust of the earth, so that if anyone could count the dust, then your offspring could be counted. Go, walk through the length and breadth of the land, for I am giving it to you."*
>
> —Genesis 13:14-17

Notice God says to "*look around from where you are... All the land that you see I will give to you and your offspring forever.*" Then in verse 17, He says, "*Go, walk through the length and breadth of the land, for I am giving it to you.*"

There are three vital steps that the Lord showed Abraham. First, look! Yes, from where you are. You may say, "Well, I do not have much." He did not say to look at what you have but from where you are. All that you see, He will give you. Oh, this is where we miss it so often. We really need to focus on allowing God to stretch our perception so we can see farther. To see **from** where we are takes imagination; otherwise, all we see is **where** we are.

WE REALLY NEED TO FOCUS ON ALLOWING GOD TO STRETCH OUR PERCEPTION SO WE CAN SEE FARTHER.

So, the first law we need to master is the law of dominion. This is the first of the nine laws for acceleration. You will never rise higher than what you can see. So let's stop and answer the question: What do you see? You will never walk toward what you do not see. Never!

God was telling Abraham, "Look, and I will give you all that." Notice He said "will give you all that," not "have given you all that." All of it was his to take, but Abraham had his part to walk out first. Unless Abraham walked it out, God had no jurisdiction over that land. He could only give him the land he set his foot on. Why? Because Abraham had the blessing, the anointing, and the jurisdiction in the earth realm to bring that land under heaven's jurisdiction.

And the last part of this equation is that you can never occupy what you do not walk out. If you do not occupy it, as I stated earlier in this book, you can never administrate it to produce a benefit in your life. Let's review.

1. What do you see?
2. What you see, you must then walk out.
3. You will never walk out what you do not see.
4. You can never occupy what you do not walk out.

The next time you are out driving around looking at houses, ask yourself a question: How did it get there? I know you may say that is a silly question. But seriously, how did it get there? Someone had to see it before it was built. From that picture, a blueprint would be drawn; then from the blueprint, an estimate of money and time would be put together to form a quote, the cost to build the house. The point I am making is someone had to see it before it was built. Someone drew what they saw and then built what they drew. And when that house was finished, it looked exactly like the blueprint.

Let me say this again:

Someone had to see it before it was built.

Someone had to draw what they saw (a plan).

Someone had to build what they drew (walk out the plan).

BUT IT ALL STARTS WITH "WHAT DO YOU SEE?" THE LAW OF DOMINION!

But it all starts with "What do you see?" The law of dominion!

I am going to ask you again, in regard to your life, "What do you see?" Actually, stop for a minute and take a few notes. Then step back from that picture and ask yourself, "Is that really what I want?" Remember, you are the one who draws the picture. My $1,500 example could have become $150,000 easily enough if I had known the price was going to go up. Someone knows if the price is going to go up, and He invites you to ask Him any time you need to.

There is a great Scripture, Romans 12:2, that I love to read from time to time:

> *Do not conform to the pattern of this world, but be transformed by the renewing of your mind. Then you will be able to test and approve what God's will is—his good, pleasing and perfect will.*

Basically, this Scripture is telling us to change our thoughts and not to conform to the pattern of life that we have used in the past. My mom would buy dress patterns so she could sew dresses for my two sisters when they were small. Now, if she had sewn a dress, then when it was finished, she hated it, then went back and used that same pattern again, she would have gotten the same dress she hated every single time, no matter how many times she made it. To have a different result, she had to change the pattern she used, and this is true for us as well.

You may say, "Well, Gary, I really do not have a pattern for my life." And I would say, "Yes, you do; it is what you think about all day long." And if you said you do not think about anything all day long, well, that is your problem.

Again, the law of dominion sets your vision. This is where you live but not how you live. This is your vision, your dominion, your future that you are embracing and preparing for—which brings up a great point. You can always tell where you are heading by what you are preparing for. If a person wants to be a great pianist, they will want to practice. If they want to succeed in their business, they will become a student of that business. So, tell me: What do you practice in your off time? I am not trying to make you feel bad, but you need to stop and face the facts. This is how it works.

One last question I want to ask is: "Where are you being dragged in life?" You will say, "Hey, Gary, no one is dragging me anywhere." Sorry to differ with you, but you are being dragged somewhere. At least that is what the Bible says.

> *When tempted, no one should say, "God is tempting me." For God cannot be tempted by evil, nor does he tempt anyone; but each person is tempted when they are dragged away by their own evil desire and enticed. Then, after desire has conceived, it gives birth to sin; and sin, when it is full-grown, gives birth to death.*
>
> —James 1:13-15

James is warning us about allowing an evil desire to drag us into temptation and sin. But any desire will drag you toward its fulfillment, good or bad. James says a person is tempted when a desire is present. You can have either a good desire or an evil desire; both will drag you toward fulfillment. Once a desire is there and you give in to enticement, a plan of fulfillment will be conceived. Once the plan is acted on, James says it gives birth to the action of fulfillment, and then comes the satisfaction of the reality of the desire. So remember, what you put in your heart, what you allow to entice you, will drag you toward its fulfillment. This concept works for you and against you, depending on the type of desire you are meditating on. What do you see?

The law of dominion:

> *Enlarge the place of your tent.*
>
> —Isaiah 54:2a

Chapter 6

THE LAW OF CAPACITY

Enlarge the place of your tent [The Law of Dominion], *stretch your tent curtains wide* [The Law of Capacity), *do not hold back; lengthen your cords, strengthen your stakes.*

—Isaiah 54:2

Now, we move on to the law of capacity. After we have increased our dominion, things have to change. What I mean is if you are going to take more territory, your ability to manage that new territory is determined by your capacity. The law of dominion spoke of "where" you live. The law of capacity speaks of "how" you live each day: your habits, your routine, and how you use your time. Here, God is saying that you need to make room for the increase that He wants to bring you. Your current tent, how you invest your time and your current ability, is too small and is not able to handle the increase of responsibility that would come with the greater territory, so something must change.

Stretch your tent curtains wide, **and don't hold back**. I love that part. Even after you think you have adjusted things to handle more, God says you are still not thinking big enough. Don't hold back; make room for a lot of growth, a lot!

So, let's dig into this law. The law of capacity simply says that when you have reached your capacity, you are done. There is no more room for growth. The tent represents how you live and the processes you use to manage your day and responsibilities.

A study I read states that 8 out of 10 employees are overwhelmed.[17] That's right; most people's days are already maxed out. Because of this, they have stopped dreaming, which goes back to law number one, the law of dominion. People who have maxed out their capacity stop dreaming. Their noses are to the grindstone, so they do not even entertain new ideas. Why? Because they can barely get done what they already must do each day.

So, let me ask you, "Are you overwhelmed? Do you wake up with dread? Are you totally exhausted?" If you are, then you are stuck, and I mean stuck. There is only one way to get unstuck and start dreaming again, and that is you must change your processes.

The only way to increase your capacity is to change your processes.

Let me give you an example of what I am talking about. Let's say you have a 100 by 100 foot plot of ground where you have planted wheat for the homemade bread you bake in your bread maker. You would probably harvest that little piece of ground with a sickle and thresh the wheat the old-fashioned way, by hand.

But let's say that you want to increase your harvest, and you decide to plant 5 acres of wheat. At harvest time, as you begin to attack that field of wheat, you work hard for a couple of hours, and when you look up, a dread comes over you as you see you have only made a tiny dent in the total acreage you have to harvest. I suppose it is still possible that you could accomplish your task, given enough time and if every other demand on your life is put on pause.

17. "8 Out of 10 Employees Feel Overwhelmed and Overworked," https://theundercoverrecruiter.com

But let's go a step further and say you wanted to start selling your wheat, and you decide to plant 10,000 acres of wheat. Now what? Well, first of all, you would probably never even entertain the idea, because you would filter that possibility through a "There is no way I could harvest that much wheat with my sickle!" mindset.

Here, we see that even the law of dominion is now put on hold by law number two, the law of capacity. Again, the law says that when you have reached your capacity, you are capped. That's it; that is all you can do. What is the answer for your capped capacity? Change your processes. You would have to change how you live in the tent, change how you live your daily life, to be able to handle that increase. In the 10,000 acre example, you would obviously have to buy a combine or two. On top of that, you would have to have employees, have an HR department, health benefits, a payroll department, plus more tractors and equipment. Let's just say that your current daily routine would definitely be changing.

Let me give you another example. Let's say you spend about four hours a week mowing grass with a hand mower. You want your sales to increase at your company, and you know if you just had the time, you could bring in more business. At the moment, though, you just do not have time. What is the solution? You have several. You could buy a zero turn mower or, better yet, you could just hire it done and spend your time making money. This simple illustration applies to any area of your life. Again, you have to change your processes to gain more capacity.

Oh, I know we all love the word change. That is a joke—most people don't—but if you want to increase your territory, you must. There is a word in the passage of Isaiah 54 that you may have skimmed over, but it carries a lot of truth.

<u>**Stretch**</u> your tent curtains wide.

It takes effort to stretch those tent curtains wide. Everything inside the tent has to be rearranged, and that applies to life as well as in the tent. Let's use a simple example. Take a new balloon and blow it up. It is usually pretty hard to blow up the first time. After you have blown up the balloon, now let the air out of it. You will notice that the balloon is not the same size as it was when it was new. It is much bigger; and if you have to blow it up again, you will find that it is much easier to do. So, what happened to the balloon? You stretched the latex into a new normal. The balloon will now stay in that newly stretched state. Putting that example into the law of capacity mindset, you have effectively increased the balloon's capacity, but to do so, you had to stretch it.

Guess what? You need stretched into a new capacity. At first it will be hard, but after a while, it becomes your new normal. Let me give you an example in my life. As you may know, Drenda and I do two daily TV broadcasts. This was something that neither one of us saw ourselves doing, and it was quite a stretch for us to even begin doing TV. Neither of us had any experience doing TV, knew nothing about how to do TV, and did not have the hundreds of thousands of dollars needed to launch into TV.

YOU NEED STRETCHED INTO A NEW CAPACITY. AT FIRST IT WILL BE HARD, BUT AFTER A WHILE, IT BECOMES YOUR NEW NORMAL.

But one day, we felt we had heard from the Lord to start doing TV. So we began the process of finding how to go about doing TV; and to be honest, the more we learned, the more we realized we had no clue. God was faithful to bring us people who did know how to do TV; and by faith, we launched our TV broadcast on two local networks in Ohio in 2007. At the time, we hired a company to come in once a month and record four or five programs, as we were airing them once a week. The airtime cost at the time was $9,000 a month, which seemed like a lot of money to come up with. Over the next year, we began to take on more networks, and our monthly airtime bill climbed to $50,000 a month. Now at that point, I will have to admit, I was just about overwhelmed; but again God was faithful, and we went on several national networks. So, yes, I was stretched way outside of my comfort zone. But I started getting comfortable with the TV production, and the money was coming in to pay for our weekly broadcast. But one day, that all changed. It was on a normal Wednesday evening prayer meeting, and my daughter Amy was leading prayer. Suddenly, she stopped, looked at me, and said the following.

"The harvest is too big for you. I am stretching you. Only by my Spirit can you understand what is about to happen. Will you step out, let me lead you to hard things beyond your understanding, the impossible?"

Wow, this wasn't my first rodeo. I knew that God was going to present me with an opportunity that was bigger than I was, and He was preparing me for it before it came. Would I say yes? Was I willing to be stretched? I knew the pain of stretching as I had already been tested by it many times, but I also understood the reward of being stretched. So that night, I said, "Yes, Lord, whatever it is, I say yes."

About a month after that prayer meeting, we received a call from the Daystar TV Network which we had a weekly time slot on. Daystar is a huge Christian TV network that broadcasts in every time zone in the world, and they offered us a daily time slot. I knew that they usually have no daily time slots available, and I also knew that if I turned it down, I would probably never have another chance at having one. But I also knew that to go daily would require a radical transformation in how we did TV, not only in the personnel and equipment but also in the finances needed to pay for it.

At the time, we were just keeping up with the cost and production of doing a weekly broadcast, and I did not see any room in our finances to take on more. We were still using a company that came in and taped and edited our weekly TV show. But then I realized that I would have to develop our own team of producers and editors, plus we did not even have the cameras and other equipment needed to go daily. There was certainly one thing that I can say I agreed with the Lord on in regard to that prophecy I received that Wednesday night. He asked if I would allow Him to lead me into the impossible. Well, I had to agree, this seemed totally impossible. To make a long story short, God brought the people and enough finances to get started, but it was tight; and I will admit, I was being stretched!

Let me help you understand what happened next. You are paying an airtime bill for a weekly, which is once a week. Then you go to a daily, which is five days a week. You have a sudden increase in expenses to five times the amount you are currently paying with the weekly, which we were only just keeping up with. However, the people at Daystar understood that and told us that we would probably fall behind paying our airtime bills at first since it would take some time for our new audience to be aware of us and to start supporting the broadcast. We signed the contract to go daily, and sure enough, we were not able to pay our first monthly bill to our media company that managed our contract with Daystar. But we all expected this, so it was not a huge deal.

But at five months down the road, we were still falling further behind in our airtime bills. I then received an email from our buyer stating that we were $500,000 behind on our bills, and their attorneys were wondering what we were going to do about that. Have you ever popped a balloon while you are blowing it up because you put too much pressure in it? Well, I felt like I was just on the verge of popping. I had no idea how I was going to pay that airtime bill, and the worst part of it was the name of my TV broadcast is *Fixing the Money Thing*. I wrestled with that one. I even told Drenda that maybe we needed to back down on the TV airtime, because we couldn't continue like that. But all she would say is, "What did God say?"

We had gone to a small prayer meeting, and without telling anyone what was going on, several of the men there felt led to pray for me. As they prayed, I suddenly felt the weight of the whole situation lift, and I knew that everything would be okay. A few days later, I had a dream in which I saw a huge stack of checks. I could see the amounts on some of the checks and many of the names on those checks. I woke up knowing that God was bringing in the money. That weekend, amazingly, we had $500,000 come in above our normal offering amount at church, which gave us the funds to get our bill paid and current.

Our media expenses have grown now to hundreds of thousands of dollars a month, yet I can sleep like a baby. Why? Because I have stepped into a new normal, a new capacity. Yes, change was a huge part of it—and at times it was not comfortable; I can tell you that—but the reward was and is worth it for sure. So let me give some advice.

Do not let your lack of capacity dictate your vision!

Let your vision dictate the changes you need to make in your capacity!

Here is a key to help you figure out your next step and what processes need to be changed. Just answer the following question.

What frustrates you about your life?

Your answer identifies where you are having trouble keeping up or areas that are not your strength where you would be better suited handing that off to someone else.

Let's say that you spend about three hours a week mowing your lawn. Is that the best use of your time? As I have already mentioned, you can change your processes by buying a faster mower or, even better, paying the kid down the street to mow it for you. **Stay in your lane**. Stay free to dream of taking greater territory.

The second question you need to answer is this.

Does your current process have the ability to match your expectations?

For instance, if I own a super big washing machine and it is capable of handling the wash for all my clothes, yet my clothes are still not getting washed, then I have a time management issue. This in itself is a process issue but a different one that we will talk about in the next chapter. But if I am washing my clothes down at the creek on a rock and I still have piles of dirty laundry at home, then I must realize that my process does not have the capacity to match my expectation or my need, in which case I would have to buy a washing machine or hire someone to wash my clothes for me.

WE ARE WORKING TOO HARD AND TOO MUCH TO SIT AND DREAM AND TO ADMINISTRATE THE PROCESSES WE CURRENTLY USE IN OUR DAILY LIVES...

Most of us, without realizing it, life a live of unfulfilled goals.

Not because we are not working hard enough, just the opposite. We are working too hard and too much to sit and dream and to administrate the processes we currently use in our daily lives, inside the tent.

For instance, I read an article that said most people waste multiple hours a day watching TV, surfing the web, or talking on their phones. I am sure you have heard someone say this common expression at the end of the day, "Where did all the time go? How can it already be time to go to bed?" Well, that is a good question and one that you need an answer for. In our next chapter, we will answer that question, because you need to know where all that time went. But for now, just know that when your capacity is capped, you really are not trying to answer that question. You just know you are behind; and instead of trying to figure out where the time went, you are focusing on how to run faster to get caught up.

One of the simplest things you can do to increase capacity is to make an old-fashioned to-do list. But most people who have a to-do list fail to accomplish what is listed. Why? Well, again, their processes are inadequate to handle the issues. Secondly, they start on the easiest items first and never get to the hard, important items. So, here is a key: Handle the hardest, most disliked but urgent items at the beginning of every day, and you will be amazed how much you can get done and how that nagging guilt of being overwhelmed leaves.

Your processes lead to a plan of completion; and if you cannot complete your plan, then that is an indicator that the process needs to change. One thing that I need to warn you about is procrastination. Do not put up with a capped capacity for a second. Always be thinking ahead and asking the Holy Spirit for help and direction. Your capacity is usually not capped suddenly without warning, although that can happen, like it did in my story. Usually, you can see it coming for a while. The problem is when we do not look forward and see it coming and then are caught off guard, and everything becomes an emergency.

I remember when our church was very small but was growing. I was extremely busy building the church and my business. At the time, I had a spare time bookkeeper running the books at the church, and I could see that we were not going to be able to continue that much longer. In desperation one night, Drenda and I held hands and prayed that God would lead us to someone who could help. It was about 10:00 the same night we had prayed, and the phone rang next to our bed. It was the wife of one of our leaders in the church. Here is what she said. "I was praying, and I felt the Lord tell me to call and ask you if you needed any help in the financial area. I have a lot of experience in the financial field, and I would love to help." Wow, we were relieved. We knew this woman was trustworthy and was very detailed in her daily life and work but did not know she had a lot of experience in bookkeeping. She became our bookkeeper and did an awesome job.

Unfortunately, Drenda and I had spent needless weeks of worry and stress trying to figure out on our own how to deal with our bookkeeping problem instead of proactively asking God for help. I remember when this woman called, she said that she knew it was late but felt the Lord told her to call at that moment. God knows all about the assignments He has planned for you, and He will help develop your capacity for those assignments before they show up.

I also want to talk for a moment about setting a proper capacity posture. I know that is a strange phrase, capacity posture. But I believe this is vital and goes with the word in Isaiah when He said to make room and do not hold back. I think most people aim way too low when setting out into a new venture or assignment.

I can remember sitting next to a guy on a plane, and we struck up a conversation. I asked him what he did, and he told me that he owned a bakery. Thinking that he probably owned a small bakery like the ones in my town that do weddings and sell cookies, I asked him about his. He told me that it was just a local bakery in Boston, and he had just opened it two years ago. I asked how it was going, and his answer shocked me. He said that they did, I think, over 20 million last year. "Wait," I said, "I thought you said you just opened this bakery two years ago." He said that was correct. I then asked him how he did over 20 million in his second year in business. He told me that his bakery did not aim at the birthday party cakes and cookies as their primary business. Instead, they aimed at big corporate accounts from day one. I realized that this guy did not start a bakery to pay his bills; he started it to become wealthy! His mindset so captured my attention and was so different than most people's.

His story is a perfect example of law number one, the law of dominion, and the law of capacity working together. When he set out to launch his business, he set his capacity at a high potential before he ever opened. He went in anticipating and expecting to go big and wanted all the machinery in place to do so. Most people slug it out with antiquated processes and just stay overwhelmed and beaten by the competition. So always set your capacity posture up front just ahead of where you think you will be.

Your processes must be duplicable. I currently have over 100 employees in the ministry, including my financial company. Early on, I often had the unpleasant experience of finding out when an employee moved on that we had lost all our processes, because no one knew how to do what that person did. No one thought to write out the processes so no matter who was in the position we would still have our processes in place. I know, a dumb mistake, but so many small companies and organizations are in the same place. Many with no clear lines of communication among their team see balls drop on important projects, which keeps them in the capacity cap and not growing or, worse, losing ground. So let me say this again:

Your processes must be duplicable!

Subway makes a good sub for sure, but it is just a sub sandwich—which I think all of us would say we could make if we just baked our own bread to bring ours up to their model. Yet, they have been able to maintain around 42,000 locations around the world, according to statista.com. Or let's take McDonald's with 39,000 stores worldwide, according to the same source. Or what about Uber, which was in over 10,000 cities worldwide in only 12 years of being in business, according to mappr.com? Did these things just happen by themselves? No, anyone can make a hamburger. The two guys that started Uber were not just looking for a better way to get to work. No, they had world domination in mind when they launched. But for these companies to grow like they did, they had to have great and well-defined processes. And I am sure they had to change them along the way.

I have been in sales all my life. Even though I am a pastor of a large church and also do daily TV, I still own my financial services company. When I started that business, all the income was produced by my personal sales with clients. I knew that if I did not have my week set up by Saturday, I would lose half of the following week's productivity. So, you guessed it, I spent most of the day Saturday on the phone setting up those appointments.

In my company, I have trained hundreds of salespeople. Most of them hoped for a great week in sales, but few had one. The reason? They hoped instead of having a plan. Most did not like making phone calls, so they procrastinated and did not get their weeks maxed out. They did not have a well laid out plan as to who they were going to call Monday morning. They only hoped that they would have success on the phone Monday morning. They also did not practice the ratios of the business, how many calls needed to be made to gain one client. So, when two people said no in a row, they would tell me that being in sales was not for them, and they would quit. But if they understood that for every 10 people they talked to they would be making, let's say on average, between $3,000 and $5,000, they would continue making their calls, knowing that a yes was just around the corner.

Drenda and I met at school in Oklahoma and started our financial services business there. It was tough learning sales as I was not an outgoing person, and I had to force myself to do the work. But after a while, I got comfortable making my calls, knowing my product, and working with clients. But one day while out jogging, the Lord told me that I was to move back to Ohio. So Drenda and I moved back to Ohio, but it was tough all over again.

I had to build my business from scratch and started out making cold calls to find my initial clients. I found that if I made 90 phone calls a day, I would get to talk to about 25 people. The others would not be home and were probably at work, but I would leave a message, which some responded to. Out of the 25 people that I actually got to talk to, only about 6 to 7 were interested and actually set an appointment. Of those 7 appointments, I would make 3 sales; and from those 3 sales, I would usually earn around $2,000 to $5,000 a week. Once I got referrals coming in, I dropped my cold calling system and simply worked with referrals. From there, I began to hire associates until I had 300 salespeople, and our office became the number 1 office out of 5,000 offices nationally.

The reason I told you this story is to emphasis that you must have a process to manage your day. Time is valuable! Today, over 30 years later, my company is still in business, except today things have changed. Our processes have changed. Today, we have software that keeps track of everything. A client can call my office, and I can pull them up in the computer and see a record of every phone call we had with them, along with what we talked about. We file every form and the sales material used on the call along with copies of every contract they have signed, as well as how these products have performed over time for them, any changes we have made, and many other items to help track our business. Today, my associates can work from home and have access to everything as well. Our clients can go online and update their plans, send us a message, or manually make changes to their data. The world is changing, and we must change as well.

And today, I do not make client calls in my business. I am much too busy to do that. I had to hand that off to the great people who run the business for me. Why? Because I have a lot of other things to do. Besides my annual board meeting, I only go into the office about once every three months; and along with checking monthly reports, I can access everything I need to keep things running. You see, I had to keep changing my processes to allow me to take more territory. Even though I do not personally meet clients today, my company still produces hundreds of thousands in net profits a year. Do I still love working with clients? Yes! Do I still love the vision of my company? Yes! But if I am to accomplish my goals, I cannot do everything. I must stay on task.

Remember, the law of capacity will either fuel your fire or cause your fire to become a smoldering has been. If you are frustrated or overwhelmed, you have already waited too long to change your processes.

...THE LAW OF CAPACITY WILL EITHER FUEL YOUR FIRE OR CAUSE YOUR FIRE TO BECOME A SMOLDERING HAS BEEN.

When your capacity is maxed out, you're done.

So don't let that happen. You may ask, "How do I know if my current processes are good or not?" Well, if you are maxed out, then they may be great processes, but you have outgrown them. Stay ahead of capacity cap by constantly evaluating your productivity, which leads us to the third law for acceleration.

CHAPTER 7

THE LAW OF OCCUPATION

Enlarge the place of your tent [The Law of Dominion], stretch your curtains wide [The Law of Capacity], do not hold back [Think Bigger]; lengthen your cords [The Law of Occupation], strengthen your stakes.

—Isaiah 54:2

Let's go back to our core Scripture for the first four laws for acceleration. The third law is based on the phrase, "lengthen your cords." If you made a tent bigger, the larger canvas area would give the wind more leverage to push the tent down. The ropes and stakes, which hold the tent to the ground, must be lengthened to gain greater leverage to withstand the pull of the canvas as more pressure is applied from the larger surface area of the canvas. But let's take a look at the ropes. They are attached to the tent, which we have said is how you live your daily life, and the stakes, which are hammered into the ground. The ground that the stakes are hammered into is back to number one, the place of your tent, your vision and dominion. The stakes are hammered into the ground to hold the ropes which hold your tent, which are your daily processes, accountable to your vision, the ground. How do they do that? Through administration! I could have called this third law the law of administration. But I chose to call it the law of occupation because you will never occupy what you do not administrate.

You will never occupy what you do not administrate! The ropes are the facts, the ROI, the details that you need to make good decisions. Administration puts the facts on the table for all to see. Since the ropes are anchored to your vision, they are holding your processes in the tent, how you live, accountable to your vision. This is how you are able to judge if your processes are able to get you to your destination.

If you travel on a British subway, you will see signs that say "Mind the Gap" at the entrance to the subway cars. If you are not mindful of the gap, you could be injured or worse by falling into the gap between the train and the landing. The same danger exists here as well. Your entire business or home life can fall apart into a big mess if you are not aware of the gap, the details. If you do not mind the gap, you are going to find yourself way off course while all along thinking things were fine.

I am a pilot, and I learned very quickly that I do not want to stray from the heading that I am following. On a very short distance from the familiar airport, I do not need to see the compass. The terrain below me is all familiar. But when I head out on a long trip, I have no reference point to know if I am heading in the right direction or not without a compass heading. So many people hope they are heading in the right direction but are actually heading the wrong way.

In my financial business, we always ask a client to work up a budget when we first meet. Obviously, if we are going to help the client get out of debt or if we are asked to safeguard their investments, we need to see where they are financially. One question we ask in that initial questionnaire is how much money they would say is discretionary each month. In other words, I am looking for money that we can work with to help them achieve their goals and get out of debt. I already know before I ask that they usually have no clue. The massive use of the modern-day credit card has eliminated the budget for most people. As long as they have any open credit available on their card, they continue to spend. But of course, this is part of the problem I am trying to expose to my clients, that they do not know, and they should.

It is always amazing to me when people tell me that they have an extra $500 or so a month, but when they do the budget, they find they are $700 in the hole every month. I had one client that said they had $1,000 extra every month but was shocked to find out that they were $1,700 in the hole every month, which was why their credit cards were all maxed out. Hmm, I wonder how that happened. Without the details, you have no way of knowing if you are going to be able to accomplish what you should be accomplishing.

More administration is required to handle all the details of your enlarged household processes. As I said before, if you were trying to harvest 10,000 acres of wheat with a sickle, people would laugh at your ignorance. You would need many combines to harvest that much. Of course, as I said, as your dominion increases, the need for your processes to change becomes more and more apparent. Moving from a hobby wheat farmer with a sickle to a massive farming operation would require everything to change. You would need a payroll department, a HR department handling HR law and employee benefits like health insurance, maintenance schedules for all the machinery you would need, and much more.

So again, if you cannot administrate it, you will never be able to occupy it.

This is what the Lord was trying to tell me in Hebrews 11:33-

34 mentioned at the beginning of the book. People are believing God to give them these great businesses and incomes, but they have no capacity to handle what they say they want.

I know of one church pastor who understands this so well. When he interviews people for a staff position, he asks them to walk him out to their car. He knows that if the car is a huge mess, then his ministry will look just like that car in a short time. He knows if they cannot administrate what they already have, there is no way they can administrate more. Now, assume he is standing at the messed-up car with French fries smashed into the carpet and junk strewn throughout the car, along with the now embarrassed potential employee. What do you think he hears? "Sorry, I have not had time to clean my car out lately." But is that really an excuse? No, sorry, nice try. There are car washes, and there are businesses who come to your home and wash and clean your car for you.

This person has a vision problem, obviously. But I will bet that when that car was new, they loved how neat and clean it was, and they were determined to keep it that way. But then life happened. Their daily processes were not able to keep up with their vision. So what happened? They compromised their vision and just accepted driving a dirty car around. In this case, once the problem was observed, a new process should have been put in place and administered to ensure that this issue did not continue. For instance, a simple to-do list reminding the owner to drive through the car wash every Wednesday on their way home from work would have worked. Or scheduling someone to clean the car for them. The bottom line was that this person dumbed down their vision to fit in their current capacity limits.

Administration has a very important role. It points out what processes need changed, as I said, but it will also point out where you personally may need to step out of the process. What I mean by that is as things get more complicated, you will need to hire professional help. I know the mindset of that possible employee with the dirty car. They are thinking, *One day, I will get to this.*

But I noticed that people who get things done are always asking, "Who can I hand this task to?" I think we all deal with the "I need to do this" mentality. This comes from our small survival thinking. Let me say it this way: You cannot afford to do all those small tasks. Your time is worth more than that.

Yes, at one time, I prepared and filed my own taxes. That was not one of my strong points for sure, and I dreaded doing it. Eventually, I was too busy, and as my returns became more complicated, I lacked the knowledge to properly do them. I realized that I should have hired that out long ago, and my delay was hurting me, not helping me. The same with payroll taxes; what a mess to personally administrate that. I thought I was saving money, but in the long run after getting a few penalties, I was not saving any money at all. Now, for one hundred dollars a month, a company does my payroll and files all my required payroll forms. That was a no-brainer!

The administration of my time is a huge part of my life. With so much going on, there is no way I could keep up on my own. I currently have two personal assistants who run my calendar and handle all kinds of things for me. When someone asks me if I could meet with them, I tell them to talk to my assistants. I would not have a clue; they run my calendar. Administration shows me where I need to replace myself so that I can focus on the big picture, the vision. So, let me make a statement that you need to remember.

Capacity is always held hostage by a lack of delegation and administration.

That statement is so important that you need to stop and read

YOU ARE THE SKINNY NECK OF THE FUNNEL, SO GET OUT OF THE WAY AND STOP TRYING TO DO IT ALONE.

it again. Better yet, write it down somewhere where you can see it often. So, here is the question: What can you delegate? You are the skinny neck of the funnel, so get out of the way and stop trying to do it alone.

As the leader, be it of a great company or of your life itself, you must lead the change in your processes along the way to ensure that you are operating at a level of capacity that will take you to your goals. Administration provides the facts to drive that change. Administration provides the details that are invaluable to you, the leader—such as your ROI on current processes, employees, marketing, and various other areas of your life. They all show you what needs to be changed. A bathroom scale is a device that puts the facts on the table (no pun intended) and helps you navigate change in your diet and exercise habits. What do you need to buy? What do you need to sell? Administration provides all the answers.

Several years ago, we had a huge ice storm in Ohio that knocked out the electricity for over a week. There were no gas stations open, no cell phone coverage; and at the time, I had no wood cut for my fireplace. I did have one room that had a propane fireplace in it, and that was where we stayed. My kids thought it was one of the greatest times of their lives as we all played games in that room throughout the week. But for me, it was a disaster that could have been avoided. I have acres of woods that are full of downed trees that should have been cut up before winter.

After that event, I did a couple of things. One, I added a freestanding 250-gallon gasoline tank to my property that I keep full. It provides the gas I use to mow the lawn in the summer, but it also serves as a backup in case of an emergency. I also added a whole house propane electric generator that is large enough to run everything in the house. And, of course, I keep the propane tank full. I also keep a good supply of cut firewood in my barn and always own at least one all-wheel drive vehicle to be sure I can get around in the winter. We keep a month's supply of groceries stored in our basement and always keep some cash on hand as well. All of these things were available before that long week of being locked in by the weather, yet I did not act on them. This is why a plan of administration will help you see things before you get there. It will point out areas of weakness that might derail your plans and sabotage your goals.

So, let's go back to that to-do list I mentioned earlier. I am glad you did get some things done on that list, but ask yourself this super important question: "Why didn't I get all of the things on the list completed?" If you are like me, there were times when something stayed on my to-do list for months. That was totally unacceptable. What did that tell me? It told me that my capacity was capped, and even if I had the greatest ideas since sliced bread, it would have made no difference. For no matter how diligent I was to put those ideas on my to-do list, they would not get done. The list would simply keep getting longer. I had to change my processes!!!! You know you have or had the same problem. Administration, the list, showed me that I was fooling myself, and change was demanded if I was serious about my vision.

Now, looking at your list, was there a way you could have delegated some of those items? Is there a way you could change your processes so that you do not have to deal with that same issue again? Wouldn't it be great to leave your office at the end of the day and know that you accomplished the entire list? It can be done. Just think how it would affect your success if your thoughts changed from *I have to remember to get this done* to *where am I headed next?* That would be HUGE!

Remember, the bigger the vision, the greater change in your processes that must take place and the greater the need for good administration. How important is the law of occupation?

> *Who faith conquered kingdoms,* ***administered*** *justice, and gained what was promised.*
>
> —Hebrews 11:33a

It might just be the difference between you wishing you were there and actually being there. Here is a fact that I know will help some, and possibly you.

Some people love administration!

I know when I talk about administration, many people's brains tilt—not all, of course, but many. I know because I am not wired for detailed administration; it sucks the life out of me. But believe it or not, some people love it, and I mean really love it! They were made to love it!

> *And God has appointed in the church, first apostles, second prophets, third teachers, then miracles, then gifts of healings, helps,* ***administrations****, and various kinds of tongues.*
>
> —1 Corinthians 12:28 (NASB)

Guess what? God made some people who are wired for detail. I am not one of them, as I said. I enjoy a certain amount of administration but not in-depth audit level stuff.

My daughter owns a marketing company, and she is at the point of being completely maxed out. She said she cannot take any more clients until she can get some help. She showed me how all 20 of her employees are a direct report to her. She knows that is not good and she must change her structure and her processes. Why? Well, besides the fact that she is maxed out, she is having to micromanage every department, which is killing her creative side. She said her creative side is what she is good at and is the talent that makes her company go. One symptom she is experiencing is fighting the emotional drain of overload. She says she goes home emotionally worn-out, and her zeal is waning. Yep, I told her that sounds like the law of capacity being maxed out, and that is one of the symptoms, emotional burnout.

After doing some research into other bigger marketing companies, she decided to call one just to ask them some questions in regard to how they do things. She wasn't sure if they would give her any advice as they could look at her as a possible competitor. It was a long shot, she said, but she was desperate. She told me she made the call, and, surprisingly, the woman she was talking to was very excited to answer her questions. My daughter found out that the woman she was talking to had personally designed the entire job structure at her company and had written all the job descriptions as well.

My daughter was so happy to hear everything the woman was saying. After a while, my daughter had a thought, *Would this woman be willing to help me design my staff structure and proper admin structure if I paid her to help?* That really was a long shot, but she asked. And amazingly, the woman said, "I would love to; I just love administration." On top of all that, she said she would do it for free. She said she had been thinking of taking some clients on the side doing exactly what my daughter was asking, and she felt this would be a good test for her idea. My daughter was beside herself with excitement. So be encouraged; there is help out there.

Some people love what you hate!

REMEMBER, YOU WILL NEVER OCCUPY WHAT YOU DO NOT ADMINISTRATE.

Do not waste time doing what you hate. Hire it out or bring in someone that has that ability and loves it. The longer you stay there doing what you hate, the more it is going to steal your joy and excitement over your journey and possibly entice you to quit.

In conclusion regarding this extremely important law for acceleration, remember, you will never occupy what you do not administrate. The law of occupation provides the data and details needed to evaluate your processes in relation to achieving your goals.

Remember to Mind the Gap!

CHAPTER 8

THE LAW OF PRESSURE

> *Enlarge the place of your tent [The Law of Dominion], stretch your curtains wide [The Law of Capacity], do not hold back [Think Bigger]; lengthen your cords [The Law of Occupation], strengthen your stakes.*
>
> —Isaiah 54:2

The law of pressure is really not hard to understand when you understand the purpose of the tent stakes. Stakes hold things in place. Simple enough. In this case, God is telling us to anchor our stakes into the vision, the place of our tent, so they do not get pulled out by the increased pressure that managing a larger tent brings. Remember, it is in the tent that the processes of daily life take place. Our increased vision now requires a change in how we live, with new and more complex processes. As long as the stakes hold, the tent will stay up and the processes in the tent will continue to morph as needed to accomplish the vision, represented by the ground that the stakes are pounded into, the law of dominion.

So, let me paraphrase the actual meaning of its application. We have already established that the ropes represent administration holding our daily processes accountable to our vision, the ground. So why would God tell us to strengthen our stakes? Because as we enlarge our tent, meaning the change or new processes demanded by our bigger vision, there will be more weight or pressure to either give up on our vision or compromise our vision due to the chaos that change brings. Change is always disruptive. We need to hold on when the ship is rocking back and forth. If we hold on and do not let go, the ship will get us to the port that we set on the compass. Sometimes change produces a rocky ride, but change is worth it. In simple terms, strengthening your stakes simply means this.

Do not let pressure cause you to compromise your vision. Don't let go!

You have the promises of God, and His Word is not going to fail. So, hold on to that vision. Increase is coming. I have talked to so many people who have regrets. They will tell me they should have stepped out when they were younger, or they wish they would have started that business, taken that trip, or built that house. The list goes on and on. Of course, looking backwards is always with 20/20 vision, but looking forward with a promise from God is better than looking backwards with 20/20 vision.

In saying that, you must remember that a promise always speaks of the end, not the beginning. God always speaks in the finished tense, meaning He is always going to speak of the conclusion or the victory in a direction or assignment. When God said to Abraham that He was going to make him into a great nation, at the time, Abraham did not even have a child. But God was speaking of the end and not the present.

YOU MUST REMEMBER THAT A PROMISE ALWAYS SPEAKS OF THE END, NOT THE BEGINNING.

I remember I had a dream one time where God showed me

that my business was going to produce a lot of money. I mean more money than I had ever thought of at the time of this dream, which was years ago. When I asked the Lord how that was going to happen, He said, "You will have to rebrand your company twice to reach that level." I was confused. I said, "I do not understand. Why would I have to rebrand my business twice and not just once?" He answered me and said, "Because you cannot see the changes that need to be made until after you rebrand the first time." What He was saying was that I couldn't see that far from where I was. And He was right. I rebranded the company, even changed its name during that first major rebranding, and the company did improve; but there were still many issues and processes that were not clear after that first rebranding and restructuring took place.

Don't get me wrong. We dealt with a lot of dysfunction in that first rebranding, but as we continued to grow more, more issues showed up. Our processes were falling behind. So we kept a list of the areas of weakness that we spotted as we grew and began planning our second rebranding and restructure. One of the areas that we were dealing with was our computer systems. At the time, every associate worked from their own laptop and then was required to upload the files to us once a month so the home office could file them. We knew that if we were going to become a strong nationwide company, we would have to go to a web-based program that could be accessed from anywhere and would save all of our needed files automatically, taking that important role out of our associates' hands.

We also needed to provide a way to speak to our clients and provide them with a better online experience while they monitored their accounts. We realized the day of the mailed-out newsletter was over; and with constantly changing tax laws and guidelines, we needed a way to communicate all of this to our clients. We also knew the day of the stuffed file cabinet was over and everything needed to be filed digitally. We needed a better way to securely file our clients' personal data forms and signed contracts, as well as track and file every client phone call and any changes or directives that were to take place after the call. All of that was being done on paper then, but we knew we would not become the company we wanted to be without changing that.

So, we rebranded the entire company a second time. This took place about seven years after the first rebranding. Remember, our company is 35 years old, and a lot has changed over that time. We started using a software platform called Salesforce, which gave us the ability to do all of these things automatically. The result of that second rebranding opened up our clogged capacity and gave us the capability to move forward and capture the territory our vision demanded. We started seeing more success than we had ever hoped for back when God first spoke that word to me. But I had to walk out that process.

The promise always speaks of the end. If you do not understand the end, the promise, and vision, you might get discouraged and quit. But as long as you keep those stakes in the ground and refuse to compromise the vision due to pressure, you will find your way through. God will show you.

When I was called to preach, I was 19 years old. It was my birthday, and I was invited to have a steak dinner at a friend's house. My friend was the only other Christian there. As we sat down to the meal, they asked me to pray over the food, knowing that I was a Christian. As I started to pray, suddenly, the anointing of God came over me and overwhelmed me. I was shocked and taken aback by it. As I sat there, it kept getting stronger until, finally, I asked if I could be excused for a moment. I stepped out the back door into the backyard, and the presence of God got even stronger.

Suddenly, I saw a picture of me standing with a Bible in my hand preaching to a group of people. I saw the room, and I noticed that it was dark outside as the curtains on the windows were open, and I could see that it was night. I saw that the people were all sitting in folding chairs, and I saw the number of people who were there, about 20 to 30. Then I heard, not audibly but up out of my spirit, these words, "I am calling you to preach my Word." I heard that statement three times, and then the anointing lifted. As I walked back into the house and sat down, every eye was on me. They asked what happened, and I said, "I think I was just called to preach." That was a very clear picture and experience regarding my future.

Some would say, "Well, did you start preaching after that?" No, I did not. God then led me to go to college. You see, I basically flunked out of high school. There was only one guy who graduated below me in my class. God knew that, although I was called, I was not ready yet. Let's be honest. If you can't write, and if you cannot communicate, you are not ready. So, I went to college, and through a lot of hard work, I finished with a 2.9 grade point average. For me, that was awesome. At that time, college was the hardest thing I had ever done in my life, and I was glad it was over.

After college, strangely, I felt God call me to work in finances, specifically selling life insurance and securities. Why would God do that? I was shy, extremely shy. I was so shy growing up that I avoided people if I could. When I started in sales, I died a million deaths. I had to force myself to make my calls and talk to people. But I got better and better at it, and eventually, I produced the number one office for my company out of 5,000 offices nationally.

It was then that God said, "Now, leave the company and launch a church, of which you will be the pastor." You see, I was not ready when God called me. I had to walk out the process of preparation. The first official night of our new church, as I was standing there teaching, I saw the same picture that I was shown the night I was called. There were the people sitting in folding chairs, the dark through the windows, the exact room. That was an amazing confirmation that I was right where God wanted me to be. This was 21 years after I had that vision at the age of 19.

You see, God gives us the promise or picture to hold on to, to keep us walking down the correct path. So, remember, God always speaks in the finished tense. So do not let go of your vision. Anchor to it, and let it speak to you along the road of life. Then you will find the reality of the picture that led you there.

I also want you to remember this fact as you run your race.

There is a finish line!

There is a goal and a reward for the hard work of change that you are embarking on. I applaud your desire to see increase and acceleration in your life. But understand there will be issues. Change is not easy.

THERE IS A GOAL AND A REWARD FOR THE HARD WORK OF CHANGE THAT YOU ARE EMBARKING ON.

I have loved to ride bicycles all my life, and I have had several of them. Seven years ago, I wanted to ride on a century ride. A century ride is riding 100 miles in one day. I will admit it was quite an adventurous goal. I had never ridden anywhere near that amount in the past, but since I was turning 60 years old, I knew that I should do it then or I might not ever do it. As I have told you previously in this book, I lived out in the country, which was a great place to ride bicycles. Drenda and I owned an old Raleigh tandem bicycle, a bicycle built for two, that we would occasionally ride around.

So, I began to talk to Drenda about doing a century ride, together, on a new tandem as our old one was really too heavy for that long of a ride. Surprisingly, she loved the idea. I was not sure she would want to sit on a bicycle seat that long. But Drenda has always been adventurous, so we set out to find a sponsored century ride that we would like. A sponsored ride is an organized ride that has stop stations for water and food set up along your route. Plus, there is help for mechanical issues you might incur as well as medical help if needed.

One day on a commercial airline flight, she saw a century ride advertised in the airline's magazine as the most beautiful bicycle ride in the world. The ride would go around Lake Tahoe, deviate to Truckee, California, then back to Lake Tahoe to satisfy the needed 100-mile course. As we were on the plane, we both saw the provided pictures, thought it looked like it would be the best ride ever, and we signed up.

We knew to get there and to make the ride, we would first need to buy a better tandem bicycle. As I said, our old, heavy tandem would not do. After looking around, we bought a gorgeous black aluminum Cannondale tandem bike the week before we were to leave.

The ride was in California, obviously, and we had planned to drive our RV there from Ohio as we could put the tandem into the storage department on the RV. We made our hotel reservations, fueled up the RV, and headed out toward California. As we finally arrived in the Lake Tahoe area after a week of driving, we were surprised. We had not realized that Lake Tahoe was completely surrounded by big mountains. I knew the pictures were beautiful, and I should have realized this, but now looking at those climbs, I was a bit concerned about our ability to actually complete the ride. But nevertheless, we were determined to ride.

As my wife stood in line to get us registered, the guy in front of her asked her if she was riding the shorter 75-mile route or the 100-mile route. Drenda said the 100-mile route and that we were riding a tandem. He then asked her how much she had been training, and she said she had ridden back home a few times. He stared at her in disbelief and told her that we would never make it. He said that he was an avid bike rider, and he was only doing the 75-mile route. About that time, the clerk registering the event asked Drenda if we were going to ride the 75-mile route or the 100-mile route. Drenda quickly looked at the guy next to her and said, "We are doing the 100-mile route."

We started out around 6:30 in the morning and really had no trouble for the first 50 miles except for a few needed bike adjustments. You see, we had actually only ridden our new bike once before we got there. I know, I know, we were totally naïve. There was one other small detail that we failed to calculate in our plans, and it was that most of our ride was between 7,000 and 8,500 feet in elevation. We had not counted on the lower oxygen at those elevations. By the 50-mile mark, I was starting to feel it, and I knew I was in trouble. But after some rest and grabbing a bite to eat, I felt better, and we started out again. The hardest part of the ride was still in front of us, an 11-mile climb just before the finish line.

It was at mile 86 and halfway up that 11-mile climb where I just could not go farther. My handlebars were white with salt from my perspiring in the hot sun, and my muscles would not work. I sat there beside the road about to call it quits when a woman came over and said, "It looks like you need salt." She could see that I was pale and the handlebars were covered in salt. She went to her car and brought out a jar of dill pickle brine, which is full of salt. She said she always packs the brine on long rides like this. She handed that jar to me and told me to drink it, which I did. Within minutes, I could feel the energy coming back into my body; and I got up and started up that mountain again.

When we reached the crest of the mountain, it was all downhill to the finish line. As I looked ahead of me, I could see it, the finish line. Nothing looked better to me at that moment than that finish line! I knew once I got there, there would be food, a hot shower, and the satisfaction of doing something that seemed impossible. We were one of only two tandems on that ride from a crowd of about 300 that rode that day. I found out later from those I talked to that riding a tandem on that ride was much harder than a one-person bike. When we actually crossed the finish line, I do not think words could express our feelings of gratitude and relief that we had finished it.

Your journey will have a resemblance to our road trip on that bike. Everything seems glorious as you start out on your journey, but there are always issues that must be navigated along the way. In our case, we would have made our trip much easier if we had done the proper preparation beforehand and had done some research on the area and the route before we went.

But the reason I told you this story is to encourage you to focus on the end, the reward, as God speaks to you about your future. Remember, He speaks of the finish line, not the beginning. How great it is going to be when you get there. So, when the road gets a little tough and you are tempted to pull up your stakes and abandon your vision, you must have a clear picture of that finish line in your mind. That was the reason you launched out in the first place, and that is what you need to make sure you hold on to. Since the Bible says to strengthen your stakes, we need to know how to do that.

Let's take a look at Habakkuk 2:2.

> *Then the Lord replied: "Write down the revelation and make it plain on tablets so that a herald may run with it."*

The first thing you must do is to write the vision down. This is not an optional play, and it is so important that it can determine if you succeed or fail. Pressure has a way of making what seemed so clear when you started out suddenly become fuzzy. Most people start looking backwards in times of pressure, when things are crazy, and there seems to be no guarantee of success. This is the time when you need to look at the vision, the end, and ask yourself, "What do I want to go back to?"

...YOU NEED TO LOOK AT THE VISION, THE END, AND ASK YOURSELF, "WHAT DO I WANT TO GO BACK TO?"

I have a friend who lost his job and was looking for answers for his life, then he found our material. He said he would listen to it every day for hours, and it began to transform how he thought. He decided to start his own trucking company instead of looking for a new corporate job. In the beginning, it was just him and a truck, but he had some success and was able to pay his bills. But as he kept listening, his vision kept growing. He began to buy trucks and then more trucks until he now has 18 trucks on the road full time. His cash flow went from $4,000 a month to over $100,000 a week in five years. He told me that it was hard and there was so much to learn about the trucking industry. He had to learn all the federal laws and then how to manage a fleet of trucks. He said there were days that he just couldn't take the chaos as the company was growing so fast. But then he would think, *Well, there is nothing to go back to, so I might as well keep moving forward.* You see, he had to stop and look forward and also realize that there was nothing behind him that he wanted to go back to.

Those stakes that Isaiah is talking about strengthening are the promises and vision that are before you. There is nothing behind you that matches the future that God has laid out before you.

Here are the steps to strengthen your stakes.

1. Write your vision down, and be sure to list why you have embraced that vision. What will life be like once you get there? What reward is waiting for you there?

2. Make the vision plain, meaning have a plan. What do you need to do to capture the vision?

3. Run with it, meaning move on it. Once you have your plan and have finished your due diligence, move on it.

4. I am adding this one: Be careful who you share your vision with and who you hang around.

The rabble with them began to crave other food, and again the Israelites started wailing and said, "If only we had meat to eat! We remember the fish we ate in Egypt at no cost—also the cucumbers, melons, leeks, onions and garlic. But now we have lost our appetite; we never see anything but this manna!"

—Numbers 11:4-6

According to the Century Dictionary, the word rabble means a tumultuous crowd of vulgar, noisy people; a confused, disorderly assemblage; <u>an ignorant mob</u>.

These folks wanted to go back to Egypt where they ate fish at no cost?! Were they blind or stupid? There was nothing back there but slavery! Hello, wake up! I know it is crazy, and I cannot understand it, but it seems people would rather turn back toward destruction than pay the price of change and freedom.

I remember a sales rep I had who was about to lose his house. Wanting to help him out, I gave him a huge list of leads that were already clients that needed to upgrade their product to a less expensive one that we had just come out with. I mean, how simple was that? You call a client and tell them that you would like to reduce their insurance rate. Remember, they were already clients of ours; it was a simple call that I am sure would have been good news. But you know what? He wouldn't do it. He said he just did not like making phone calls. Are you kidding? He was one of my sales reps. He already knew how to do that and could do it in his sleep. So, he did nothing as his house went into a sheriff's sale.

Unfortunately, he is not the exception. I have seen this over and over again with salespeople. It is a funny thing. A person will work eight hours a day at a job, but when you offer them a chance to make five times their income, along with being free, they won't work two hours a day. Is slavery that good? No, of course not. You need to remember that when there is pressure.

And pick your friends wisely; birds of a kind flock together.

You want to be around people that are going forward themselves and are encouraging you to do the same. Stay away from people who are negative and have a bad attitude toward life.

Make a concrete decision not to turn to the right or the left once you hear God and set out for your destination. Hold firmly to what God said. I have had times where I thought I would wither from the pressure. I told you in the last chapter about going on TV daily and how I had to wrestle with what God said when I had no answers. I had to hold firm to His promise and not be moved.

> *For God has not given us a spirit of fear, but of power and of love and of a sound mind.*
>
> —2 Timothy 1:7 (NKJV)

You can do it. Dig those stakes deep into the ground. Increase is coming. You are not a slave. You stand as a son or daughter in the house of God, and you have inherited access to the whole estate. All of it is available to you!

Remember, if the stakes slip, the whole tent comes down!

CHAPTER 9

THE LAW OF STRATEGY

The law of strategy is our fifth law for acceleration. And you can guess how important this law is—SUPER IMPORTANT! The definition of the word strategy, according to freedictionary.com, is a long-term plan for success, or a plan. I mentioned in a previous chapter the need to have a blueprint before you could expect to see a house built. This principle holds true for every area of life. If you were going to apply for a business loan, the first thing the banker would want to see would be your business plan. He will evaluate your plan to see if it makes sense, if he thinks it will work. A lot of people dream of going somewhere in life but have no plan to get there. I talk to people all the time, ask them what they want to do, and they will give me this lofty sounding vision. Then I will ask them how they are going to pay for it, and they have no idea; they have no plan. What is the answer? Write this down:

Once you have the plan, you have everything!

Let me give you a couple of examples of what I mean. What if I told you that I could solve all your financial issues with my next bit of advice? That what I am about to tell you will literally set you financially free, so please get your paper and pen ready to write this down? Okay, here it is: Make a net income of $10,000,000 this year. Of course, there are some people where that would not solve all their problems, but for most Americans, it would do the trick.

As I use this example in my conferences, everyone begins to laugh like it is some kind of joke. But I am not joking. If they made that amount of money this year, for most people, that would change their lives. As I explain this in my conferences, they continue to snicker and laugh, but why? They laugh because they cannot see themselves ever making that kind of money, and for them, it seems ridiculous to consider that. The problem is they cannot see themselves in that picture.

But what if I told you that I owned an export company, and I really needed some help? My company manufactures a unique product, and I need to ship 5,000 of them out right away. So, I offer you a contract to help me box and ship these items. I offer to pay you $500 for every box you load and seal for delivery. Assuming you could do 100 a day, I would be paying you $50,000 a day. And just to make my analogy a little clearer, let's say I give you a three-year contract at the same rate. Now, after signing my contract, if I told you to make a net income of $10,000,000, you would think that it was easy because you would know that it would only take you 200 days to make that $10,000,000. There would not be any sneers this time.

So, what was the difference between the folks who laughed at that suggestion and the ones that I hired to package and ship for me? The difference was a plan. Once you have the plan, you have it all. Why would I say that? Because even though you may not have the entire $10,000,000 paid out to you yet, being on the job for only a few days, you know you already have the $10,000,000 by contract if you will just follow the plan. That is why I said, "Once you have the plan, you have everything."

When Drenda and I were in horrible debt, I knew of no way out of the financial mess that we were in. We were up to our eyeballs in debt with no way out. We had IRS liens, pawnshop loans, 10 maxed out and canceled credit cards, and 3 finance company loans at 28% interest. We owed our dentist, the dry cleaners, our parents, and our friends. You name it, we owed them. In the natural, there was no hope. My financial sales business had not been going well, and I had no answers for my financial problems. As we learned more and more about the Kingdom, we knew that God was going to show us the way out.

Then one night, God gave me a dream and showed me in that dream that I was to leave the company I had been with for the previous nine years and start my own company. Now get this: My company would be helping people get out of debt! I know. Crazy, right? I mean if I knew how to get out of debt, I would have done it years before. But that is exactly what He said to do. I was a little in shock, actually, and had no idea how to start my own company. But a company helping people get out of debt? Hey, I still needed someone to tell me how to do that!

As I began to pray about this, I had a life-changing experience with the Holy Spirit in regard to just how this could happen. It happened at one of my client calls for my insurance business. Oh, I forgot to tell you that I was in the financial services industry selling insurance and securities while all this financial mess happened. I know, it is kind of like the plumber with the leaky faucet taking care of everyone else's problem but neglecting his own. Although I was slowly failing in my financial services position, the experience I had gained in my general knowledge of that field over the previous nine years was very important to what God was about to show me.

As I was sitting down with my client and his wife at their kitchen table, we went through the usual presentation, which took a snapshot of where they were financially by asking various questions and filling out what we called a data sheet. This data was primarily used to determine just how much life insurance they should have and to examine investment alternatives. As we were going through their list of debts, they both became upset, and the wife began to cry as they described how hopeless they both felt. They were both working full-time jobs and were falling short every month.

Now, after living that way for nine years myself and with God beginning to teach Drenda and me about the Kingdom, you can imagine how I felt for them. Like Drenda and I, they were Christians but with no knowledge of how the Kingdom operated. At the time, I really could not explain much about the Kingdom except some of the initial things God had already showed us. I shared those with them, and, of course, I shared some of the amazing stories we had seen happen in our own situation. Obviously, I could tell that life insurance was not their major problem. I spent some time explaining what God was teaching me concerning the Kingdom, but I longed for something I could do to also offer real financial answers regarding their situation.

At the office that night, as I was wrapping up my day and sorting through my normal pile of files and messages that I needed to return, I suddenly had the thoughts: *What if I look past the life insurance issue and take a long look at their entire financial picture? Is there anything I can do? What if I begin to look for money?* What I meant by that was, what if I could find cheaper ways of doing things that they were already doing? My goal would be simple, to find cheaper ways of doing things they were already doing and then apply any money I found to their cash flow and debt. It sounded like a simple proposition, but I really did not know much about any other financial field outside of life insurance and securities. And I need to tell you that this was before the days of the Internet. The research that I would need to do would be made the old-fashioned way, by phone and the yellow pages.

I worked on that the entire week as I was scheduled to meet this client again the following week. I was surprised by just how much money I could free up a month as I took the time to really dig into each financial area. By the time I was finished, the amount added up to hundreds of dollars a month. With my financial calculator, I added up all of their debts and then applied the freed up money to their normal monthly payments. When I hit the compute button, I just stared at the answer on the screen—6.2 years. The answer of 6.2 years was the total time it would take for my client to pay off all of his debts, including his home mortgage, without changing his income. Yes, you read that right, without changing his monthly income. I was shocked and convinced I had made a mistake, so I did the math over and over again until I was convinced that I had the right answer. Could this be? Why didn't everyone know this?

I quickly grabbed a few other clients' files I had on hand and did a quick scan of them and found the same results. Every one of them could be out of debt in 5 to 7 years, including their mortgage, without changing their monthly income. It was getting late at the office then as I finished up my calculations, but as I headed home, I was excited. If what I found was true, and all my calculations indicated that it was, then this was big, really big.

I was curious how my client might respond to this kind of information. For my upcoming appointment, I decided to type up the numbers into a simple one-page presentation. My objective was simply to give them hope; there was nothing in it for me. I knew that a possible life insurance sale was unlikely. But I also knew they would want to hear what I had found out. The following week, I again reviewed my calculations and was sure I was right.

As I rang the doorbell, I felt nervous anticipation. As I sat down at their kitchen table, I told them what I had done all week with their numbers. I slowly walked them through the numbers I had typed up, explaining how I had come up with the freed up cash along with any company name and number that would be needed to implement what I had shown them. I could tell that they were getting excited as the freed up cash kept growing. But when I came to the conclusion of being completely out of debt in 6.2 years, including their home, on their current income, they both began to cry, this time with joy. They sat there with tears streaming down their faces and just kept saying how shocked they were at the results. They jumped up and gave me a hug, and we had a great time of celebration that night.

Let's be honest. Is the IRS going to tell you how to pay less taxes? Is the banker going to tell you how to avoid paying interest? No, the whole system is designed to take your money, not protect it. I knew that what I had discovered needed to be taught to every family in America! That night had a dramatic impact on me, and I wanted to do the same thing for every client I met. So, armed with that information and with the confirmation of the dream God gave me, I left the life insurance company that I worked with, and Drenda and I launched our own company doing just what I had done for that client.

In those early years, we called our company "Faith-Full Family Finances." The name clearly said what we were all about—if you understood the Kingdom and faith, your finances would be full. I agree it was not a very good name for a company, try saying it 10 times in a row, but it worked. We later changed the name to

Forward Financial Group, which it is today, and it is still going strong.

To be honest, personally, our finances were not yet full. We still had all those debts to pay, but we knew we had found our track to run on. As we launched out with our new company, we were excited and a bit nervous at the same time. We had a lot to learn about setting up and running a company, but the biggest hurdle we faced was how to make any money doing it. Our challenge was we felt we could not, and we did not want to charge people money to help them get out of debt. This was a big hurdle, and we spent quite a bit of time praying about it and looking at options. Without going into detail, the Lord showed us an amazing strategy to set up the company and posture it to make money without charging the client a fee.

Next, we had to find a way to speed up the lengthy hand calculations I was doing with my clients' data. I knew that I would have to custom write a computer program to do what we were doing, but I knew nothing about computers or how to find someone who had the ability to do that. Again, God did some amazing work. I received a call from a person a long way from our home who had heard of us. He wanted to see what we did as a client. He loved what we did, and as we were talking, I found out that he was a computer programmer and had his own company on the side part time. I talked to him about our need, and he very enthusiastically said he wanted to help us with what we were doing. I told him that we were just starting our company and I did not have the funds yet to pay for the work he had offered, even though he had offered his work at a huge discount. He still wanted to do the work and said I could pay him whenever the money came in. So that is what we did.

People loved our business. After all, why not? It was free, and people liked finding money and getting out of debt. The business took off in a big way, and we were able to become debt free in two and a half years. Soon, we had over 300 sales representatives sharing our plan all over the country. Our company grew and has enabled us to give hundreds of thousands of dollars away to support the Gospel and people over the years.

The "debt plan," as we call it, is still produced for free today, over 30 years later. The company grew in its mission as the years went by. We went on to focus on retirement investing after the 2001 financial crash and then, of course, the 2008 crash, where millions of people lost 50% to 80% of their retirement savings. We researched safe investing options and launched that aspect of our business in 2001.

I am proud to say that of the over one hundred million dollars we currently manage for our clients, not one of them has lost one penny in their investments over the previous 21 years of financial chaos in our country and the world. And like with our debt plan, there is no fee, no administration fee or broker fee, involved initially or yearly for our investment clients. If you are tired of gambling with your retirement money, you can reach Forward Financial Group at 1-(800)-815-0818 or Forwardfinancialgroup.com for more information.

But the point I am making is that God gave us our plan. I knew that night when that client jumped out of his chair in tears and ran around the table and hugged me that I had found my answer, my plan. Of course, we had some things to work out and create to be able to monetize and produce our plan effectively for our clients. And then, of course, we needed to hire and train others to do the same thing, along with office staff. But I have never been more excited, even after all these years, than I was that first night with that client. Why? Well, of course I was excited for them, but I knew—I mean I knew—this was it. This was my plan, the path of escape for my family and me.

Once I had the plan, I knew the battle was over. It was just a matter of walking it out!

Amazing, isn't it, that one simple idea from the Holy Spirit changed our lives forever?! Yes, we had to walk it out, but God showed us where to walk. How did it feel, Gary, to be out of debt? Peace! Rest! Think about it. We went from being in severe financial dysfunction to being completely out of debt, paying cash for our cars, our home, and everything else we needed. For nine long years, I was under extreme pressure every minute of every day. I had no rest. It did not matter what day of the week it was or if it was a holiday. I was not at peace. My financial issues followed me everywhere I went. I endured constant embarrassment and humiliation due to our financial condition. Fear was my constant companion, panic attacks and antidepressants a way of life at the height of my despair. But then I was free!

Okay, Gary, I get it, and I am glad for you. But how do I get my plan, the strategy for my life? Well, I am glad you asked. I am going there next. We will start in Luke chapter five.

> *One day as Jesus was standing by the Lake of Gennesaret, the people were crowding around him and listening to the word of God. He saw at the water's edge two boats, left there by the fishermen, who were washing their nets. He got into one of the boats, the one belonging to Simon, and asked him to put out a little from shore. Then he sat down and taught the people from the boat.*

> *When he had finished speaking, he said to Simon, "Put out into deep water, and let down the nets for a catch."*
>
> *Simon answered, "Master, we've worked hard all night and haven't caught anything. But because you say so, I will let down the nets."*
>
> *When they had done so, they caught such a large number of fish that their nets began to break. So they signaled their partners in the other boat to come and help them, and they came and filled both boats so full that they began to sink.*
>
> *When Simon Peter saw this, he fell at Jesus' knees and said, "Go away from me, Lord; I am a sinful man!" For he and all his companions were astonished at the catch of fish they had taken, and so were James and John, the sons of Zebedee, Simon's partners.*
>
> *Then Jesus said to Simon, "Don't be afraid; from now on you will fish for people." So they pulled their boats up on shore, left everything and followed him.*
>
> —Luke 5:1-11

Here is what I want you to see in this story. First of all, they were professional fisherman, yet they had fished all night and caught nothing. But Jesus comes along and borrows their boat to preach from and then tells Peter, "*Put out into deep water, and let down the nets for a catch.*" Peter and his two partners, James and John, are amazed at the catch of fish they then had. It was so large that it almost sank both of their boats.

So, let's answer a question: How did they catch those fish? They had already tried all night and caught nothing, but then suddenly, they had the largest catch of their entire career. How? Here is the answer. Jesus told Peter where to fish! He said to "*Put out into the deep water.*" If Jesus shows you where to fish, you could catch fish too. Anyone could catch fish!

If Jesus tells you where to fish, you could catch fish!

Listen, the days of trusting in your own plans and strategies are over. I tried that for nine long, hard years. But it only takes one idea from God, one God-given strategy, a plan, to change your life forever. I mean, look at me. I was hopeless until God gave me that one idea to start a business that has made me millions. I am not that good. And I am sure that if Peter was standing here telling you about the huge catch of fish he had that day, he would say that he wasn't that good either. So, when I am talking about the law of strategy, I am not talking about you figuring it all out, no. I am talking about hearing supernatural strategies by the Holy Spirit. Remember what God told Abraham? "I will make you."

IT ONLY TAKES ONE IDEA FROM GOD, ONE GOD-GIVEN STRATEGY, A PLAN, TO CHANGE YOUR LIFE FOREVER.

So how do we hear those strategies by the Holy Spirit? The same way that Peter did on that boat.

Well, Gary, Jesus is not here, but it sure would be nice if He were. He could tell me what to do. I agree He is not here in person, but He is here. He has sent the Holy Spirit to speak on His behalf and help you.

> *But the Helper (Comforter, Advocate, Intercessor—Counselor, Strengthener, Standby), the Holy Spirit, whom the Father will send in My name [in My place, to represent Me and act on My behalf], He will teach you all things. And He will help you remember everything that I have told you.*
>
> —John 14:26 (AMP)

Yes, Jesus is still your Counselor and help through the Holy Spirit. He will speak to you and show you the way to go.

But if you are going to lead a life full of Holy Spirit strategies and Holy Spirit led victories, you need to be first born again and then, secondly, baptized in the Holy Spirit. If this is something totally foreign to you, that's all right. I will walk you through it. But let me get right to the point: Jesus said it was so important to be baptized with the Holy Spirit that He said you shouldn't leave home without it! I did not say that; Jesus did in Acts 1:4-5.

> *"Do not leave Jerusalem, but wait for the gift my Father promised, which you have heard me speak about. For John baptized with water, but in a few days you will be baptized with the Holy Spirit."*
>
> —Acts 1:4b-5

> *"But you will receive power when the Holy Spirit comes on you; and you will be my witnesses."*
>
> —Acts 1:8a

Notice Jesus said, "Don't leave home without this—this is essential!" Basically, He was saying, "You need this power to do the works of God, to be a witness for the Kingdom." Yet today, there are multitudes of Christians who have yet to hear of or experience the Baptism of the Holy Spirit. Multitudes of Christians who have been raised in church have still never heard of the need for the Baptism of the Holy Spirit. Or they were raised in church and were told that the Baptism of the Holy Spirit isn't for today, that miracles have passed away.

I was raised in a church like that and never heard of the Baptism of the Holy Spirit. I get so many emails from people all over the world who have yet to hear of this powerful truth as well. Many of the emails I receive question the validity of this gift for today, which is why I have taken the time to put on paper the truth concerning the Baptism of the Holy Spirit. This Baptism of the Holy Spirit is the key to your ability to hear unique, supernatural strategies from the Holy Spirit.

I believe the Bible is very clear concerning this area, and I want to let the Bible speak for itself. It will answer all of your questions. But first, I want to give you some background on how I discovered the truth about the Baptism of the Holy Spirit.

When I was younger, I was hungry for God (still am although I am older), and I attended a denominational church. We went through the normal religious routines on Sunday morning. Maybe you did too. I remember a couple of hymns followed by a silent moment of meditation. We always quoted the Lord's Prayer, and then the pastor gave a sermon, a closing hymn, and a benediction. Every service was laid out the same way.

The people there were wonderful, and, yes, they really loved God. But I never saw the reality of the Gospel. I didn't see people's lives dramatically changed or people healed by the power of God. I guess I could say that I didn't see a lot of demonstration of the Kingdom of God.

So there I was hungry for God, 18 years old, and running my dad's pizza shop. One night, a guy came into the pizza shop and invited me to a revival. It was being held at a small Methodist church, and the guest speaker was an evangelist who spoke about Jesus doing the same things today as He did in the Bible.

Now that caught my attention, because I wanted to see that. A couple of my friends attended this church, so I decided to visit the revival. Although I didn't hear about the Baptism of the Holy Spirit that night, I was deeply touched by the presence of God in that service. My friends that were attending there encouraged me to come back on a Sunday, which I did. I fell in love with that church and made it my new church home.

A few weeks after the revival, I met a group of women who attended the church and also held a weekly Bible study. They were talking about something called the Baptism of the Holy Spirit, the gifts of the Spirit, and various other things I had never heard of before. I was so eager to hear about this power they spoke of that I asked them if I could come to their women's Bible study. Their Bible study was in the mornings, and since I worked at night in the pizza shop, I decided to attend.

When I got there, I found out that I was indeed the only guy there and the only 18-year-old as well, but that didn't matter to me. I went to the Bible study because I was hungry for God. I asked *so* many questions.

They were so patient with me and took me through the Scriptures and showed me in my *own* Bible that the Baptism of the Holy Spirit was for today and that the power of God is available today just as it was when Jesus walked the earth. The best part was when they said it is for *all* believers—it's for anyone who asks.

After I had attended the Bible study for a couple of weeks, they told me that a national ministry called Women's Aglow was holding a citywide meeting. Women's Aglow was and still is an organization that teaches a lot about the Baptism of the Holy Spirit. These women were planning to attend, and they invited me to go with them. In those days, people from all denominations would gather to hear about and enjoy this baptism that, up until that point, was mainly talked about only in the Pentecostal churches. Those were the days many people call the Charismatic

Renewal, where this teaching of the Holy Spirit crossed over all denominational lines.

When I attended the Women's Aglow meeting, I saw that hundreds of ladies had gathered. Again, I was in the minority as a man, but there was a presence of God in that room that was tangible. That day, the speaker asked anyone who wanted to receive this gift of the Holy Spirit to come forward for prayer at the end of the meeting. So I went forward to have the ladies pray with me. As they prayed, I found myself overwhelmed as the presence of God got even stronger. As I yielded to His presence, I was amazed to hear myself actually begin to pray in the Holy Spirit and speak out words that I did not understand. I prayed in tongues for quite a while that night, so overwhelmed by the experience.

I wanted to tell everyone I met about what had happened to me! But when I shared with my friends at church what I had experienced, they weren't so excited. They would usually say that tongues were of the devil or that it had passed away. They warned me to stay away from those holy rollers!

In those days, churches weren't open to the gifts of the Spirit, and the prevailing doctrine was that miracles had passed away with the apostles. But I understood then that God's power hadn't passed away at all!

Just before this Women's Aglow event took place, I had been put in charge of the youth in that small Methodist church. There really wasn't that much required of me except that we would have a youth meeting every Sunday night in the church basement. We would usually play some games, have refreshments, and have a brief Bible study. I was really just a youth myself, but they saw that I had a zeal for the things of God and was willing to help out.

There were usually about 15 kids in the group, and after my

experience that day at the Women's Aglow meeting, I wanted to tell them about this Baptism of the Holy Spirit I had experienced. I realized that, like me, most of them hadn't even heard of this experience, and I knew that they weren't going to hear about it during Sunday morning service at that particular church.

Before I tell you what happened next, I think I should give you a quick update on my mindset at the time. I didn't get the pastor's permission to talk about this with the youth. (I now realize that I should have.) I also didn't tell him what had happened to me either.

I wasn't trying to walk in rebellion against my church, and I wasn't trying to go around my pastor. I was just excited. At that time, I really didn't understand the controversy over this topic, and I certainly didn't think the pastor would be against it.

The Sunday night after I received the Baptism of the Holy Spirit, I planned to tell the youth about what had happened to me, and to show them some of the Scriptures that talked about it in the book of Acts. We were in the church basement just sitting on the floor in a circle when I shared my experience with them and went through some of the Scriptures verifying the experience.

This particular evening, the pastor came to the meeting and was sitting on my left as I shared. I thought nothing of my pastor being there. As my pastor, I thought he already knew everything I was going to share anyway.

So, I shared with them about the meeting I had gone to and about the things I saw. I didn't really go into much detail about speaking in tongues. Instead, I focused my attention on Acts 1:8 where it says we will receive *power* when the Holy Spirit comes upon us to be witnesses for God. At the end of the meeting, I really didn't know how to end my lesson, so I just asked the kids to raise their hand if they wanted to receive the Baptism of the Holy Spirit.

I didn't know what to do at that point. I mean, I had never seen anyone minister to someone about the Baptism of the Holy Spirit except what I had seen at the Women's Aglow meeting. I think I might have known only two or three Scriptures referring to it at the time.

So, I just said, "If you would like to receive this free gift of the Holy Spirit, just raise your hand, and let's bow our heads and pray." That's really all I said. I didn't touch them or coach them on how to receive the Holy Spirit. We bowed our heads and prayed. Of course, we closed our eyes to pray like all "good" denominational Christians were taught.

As I sat there after, I said, "Amen." I began to hear some commotion among the kids. I opened my eyes and saw that some of the kids were crying, some were shaking, and seven kids had started speaking in tongues. As they started speaking in tongues, I saw the most unusual glow on their faces. They were lit up like light bulbs! I was shocked!

My pastor, who had said nothing up until this point, quickly tapped me on the shoulder and asked if he could talk to me right away. We walked into the next room, and he looked me in the eye and said, "This is of the devil. You can't be the youth leader here anymore. We're not going to have this."

I thought, *How can you say it's of the devil? I mean look at these kids! They're glowing!* You could see the anointing physically on them. Of course, I didn't even know what the word *anointing* was back then. I just knew that they were glowing, and I hadn't touched them or told them how to act. It was very discouraging and confusing to me to have my pastor rebuke me like that, and I didn't know what to do.

The next Sunday, I made my way back to church, but instead

of sitting up near the front of the church where I usually sat, I sat in the back. I knew I was kind of in the doghouse with my pastor because of the youth meeting, and I thought I had better lay low for a bit while I figured things out.

During the Sunday morning service, there was the usual silent moment of meditation. This was a very respectful and quiet moment of prayer in my church. Everyone's head was bowed, and there wasn't a sound in the church. You could hear a pin drop. It was at this very moment that I felt someone tap me on my shoulder. I was on the end of the pew, and apparently, someone was standing up in the aisle and tapping me on my shoulder.

At first, I was shocked to think that someone was up walking during the very quiet and reserved moment of prayer. When I looked up, I was surprised to see one of the kids who had been in the youth meeting the week before. I also knew that he was one of the seven that had received the Baptism of the Holy Spirit that night. He looked at me and said, "Let's go!" I thought, *Let's go? Let's go where?*

Amazingly, he was glowing just like he had been the night he had received the Holy Spirit, and I knew God was doing something. But I wasn't sure this was the time or place to do anything since I was already in trouble with the pastor. I also knew that we couldn't just do anything we wanted to in Sunday morning church.

That's when he said, "I'm going to go pray for my mom." Then, I was beginning to understand what was going on. I knew his mother. She was a small, thin woman and had been sick for a very long time. She had five vertebrae in her back that had deteriorated, and the doctor's only hope was to fuse them together. This surgery was very serious, and my friend was her only child. Of course, he was concerned for his mother.

After receiving the Baptism of the Holy Spirit, he felt sure that Jesus would heal his mother. So when he said, "Let's go," I thought he was going to go up there and lay his hands on his mom and pray for her quietly. But that's not what he did. He went up to his mother, picked her up right off the pew, and carried her to the front of the church.

He sat her down and began to pray for her as loud as he could in tongues. Now remember, this all took place during the "silent" moment of meditation, which wasn't so silent anymore. I was shocked! Then he turned to me and said, "You explain what's going on."

Then I understood why he had me come along. He figured I was the one who had told him about the Baptism of the Holy Spirit, so he figured that I could tell the congregation about it after they heard him praying in tongues for his mother.

So there I was standing in front of the congregation as his spokesman, and there he was praying for his mom in tongues. I really didn't know what to say, especially since my pastor sat there glaring at me. I simply told the congregation that his mother had been sick and that he was praying for her in tongues, which was in the Bible. But you know what? She was instantly healed that morning in church!

That was the faith of a son who really didn't care what anyone else thought about him praying. He was convinced that the Holy Spirit was alive and well and could heal his mother.

Even though she was instantly healed, the church didn't receive it. In fact, many of them came to me afterwards and said, "Well, I didn't mind him praying for his mom, but those tongues, we can't handle that tongues thing." Well then, I can guarantee that the devil hates praying in tongues as well. I hope to help you understand why he hates tongues before this book is over.

Maybe you've grown up in a church where tongues and the gifts of the Spirit weren't practiced. Or maybe you grew up being taught that tongues were not for today or had passed away. These questions aren't hard to answer. The Bible is very clear on this subject. So, let's take a good look at the Word and find out the truth on the Baptism of the Holy Spirit. Let's go back to the verse we read at the beginning of this chapter.

> *"Do not leave Jerusalem, but wait for the gift my Father promised, which you have heard me speak about. For John baptized with water, but in a few days you will be baptized with the Holy Spirit."*
>
> —Acts 1:4b-5

There are a several important points we can see in this verse:

1. The Baptism of the Holy Spirit is different than being baptized in water.

2. Jesus said it was extremely important. In fact, He made it clear that you wouldn't be able to do anything without it.

Remember, Jesus had just told the disciples to go and preach the Gospel to every nation, but they wouldn't be able to demonstrate or verify the Kingdom of heaven without this baptism. So He said, "Stay put until you receive this empowering."

> *"But you will receive power when the Holy Spirit comes*

> *on you; and you will be my witnesses in Jerusalem, and in all Judea and Samaria, and to the ends of the earth."*
>
> —Acts 1:8

Power! The Greek word for *power* here is *dunamis* and is where we get our word for dynamite. So we see that God's power comes on us to do His works. Earlier in Jesus's ministry, He had mentioned that the power, or that anointing He was operating under, was from His Father.

> *"The words I say to you are not just my own. Rather, it is the Father, living in me, who is doing his work."*
>
> —John 14:10b

> *"Very truly I tell you, the Son can do nothing by himself."*
>
> —John 5:19b

You see, Jesus needed that empowerment of the Spirit of God Himself. The word *anointing* means to "apply to." Jesus received that anointing at the River Jordan from His Father when the Holy Spirit came on Him in the form of a dove.

It was only after Jesus received that anointing that He was able to do the works of the Kingdom. If *Jesus* needed it, we need it too! That power will testify (or give witness) through demonstration that God is real to those who don't know Him.

The Bible also says that you will receive power when the Holy Spirit **COMES ON YOU**, not when He comes *in* you as when you're born again.

Many are confused when we talk about the Baptism of the Holy Spirit, thinking that they've already received the Holy Spirit when they accepted Christ. And the truth is they *did* receive the Holy Spirit when they received Christ. The Holy Spirit made their spirits alive to God and one with God.

We are alive to God by the power of the Holy Spirit on the inside when we're born again. But notice that this Scripture says when the Holy Spirit comes <u>on</u> you. This is an important fact: being born again and being anointed or baptized by the Holy Spirit are two different events. We can get a better understanding of this if we look at John 20.

> *Again Jesus said, "Peace be with you! As the Father has sent me, I am sending you." And with that he breathed on them and said, "Receive the Holy Spirit."*
>
> —John 20:21-22

We see Jesus here after His resurrection as He greets His disciples, breathes on them, and tells them to receive the Holy Spirit. This is the moment that they are born again and their spirits come alive to God on the inside. Yet Jesus tells them to wait for the Baptism of the Holy Spirit, which will come upon them at a later time.

If they had received all of the Holy Spirit when Jesus breathed on them, why would He tell them to wait in Jerusalem until they received the Holy Spirit that was promised to come upon them? These are two different events and two different functions—but the same Spirit. Again, I want to point out that Jesus had to be baptized by the Holy Spirit to enter into and be effective in His ministry as well. Before Jesus was baptized by the Holy Spirit, there is no record of Him doing one single miracle. Did Jesus multiply bread at the supper table when He was growing up? Did

He do miracles when He was a baby? Did He multiply His baby food when it ran out because He was still hungry? No! He didn't. Why didn't He? The simple and honest answer is: He *couldn't*.

It wasn't until *after* He received the Holy Spirit at the River Jordan that He began to do miracles. You see, Jesus came as a man. He didn't come as the Son of God in His power and glory. As a man, He was limited as any man is limited. He couldn't heal or do any miracles, just as you and I can't do any miracles in and of ourselves either.

However, unlike us, Jesus's spirit was not dead to God when He was born as a baby. His spirit was always alive to God; He didn't need to be born again as we do. However, although His spirit was alive to God as a son, He still needed to be baptized by the Holy Spirit before He could begin His ministry, just as we do.

> *As soon as Jesus was baptized, he went up out of the water. At that moment heaven was opened, and he saw the Spirit of God descending like a dove and alighting on him. And a voice from heaven said, "This is my Son, whom I love; with him I am well pleased."*
>
> —Matthew 3:16-17

Remember, we think of Jesus as King of kings and the Lord of lords, but this isn't the position from which He ministered. It was only after the Holy Spirit came upon Him at the Jordan River that the miracles began.

Your ministry (because *every* believer is called to do the works of Jesus) can't begin until you are baptized with the Holy Spirit—you need the power of the Holy Spirit to get things done. And you need the ability to pray in the Spirit to know how to do them.

Of course, you can offer the born-again experience by telling others what the Bible says about salvation. A lot of Christians who aren't baptized in the Holy Spirit are effective in sharing the Good News of the Gospel, but they don't have the power to demonstrate the Kingdom as Jesus did. This causes a lot of weak preaching.

When Jesus confronted the Pharisees concerning their unbelief, He made reference to the miracles He was doing. He said,

> *"Believe me when I say that I am in the Father and the Father is in me; or at least believe on the evidence of the miracles themselves."*
>
> —John 14:11

Jesus was basically saying that this demonstration of the Kingdom puts a stop to all arguments; the issue is settled. Now, of course, every believer has full legal rights to everything Jesus paid for, including healing. Every believer can receive every promise of God by faith (agreement with heaven), and they do not need the Baptism of the Holy Spirit to receive from God.

But for that power to flow from you to others, and for you to flow in the gifts of the Spirit and to enjoy the benefit of walking in heavenly mysteries through praying in tongues, you must have the power of that anointing!

You may ask, "Why should I pray in tongues?" The devil hates believers who know how to pray in the Spirit (in tongues), and I want to be sure you understand why.

When Paul said that he was glad that he prayed in tongues more than anyone else, there must have been a reason he felt that way. Paul made a comment in 1 Corinthians 14 that we need to read.

> *He who speaks in a tongue* ***edifies*** *himself, but he who prophesies* ***edifies*** *the church.*
>
> —1 Corinthians 14:4 (NKJV)

Let's dig a little deeper. What does it mean to be edified? Edified means "to instruct or benefit, especially morally or spiritually; uplift."[18]

You would have to agree that there are many times when you need instruction, to know which way to go, to understand a situation, or to make the right decision. This is what praying in tongues can help you with, to edify you, or to bring instruction to your life. Paul makes this point clear.

> *For the one speaking in a tongue is not speaking to people, but to God—for no one hears, but he speaks mysteries with his spirit.*
>
> —1 Corinthians 14:2 (DLNT)

Again, Paul speaks of our spirits as having the ability to speak out things that we have never seen, heard, or had knowledge of, or as Paul says "mysteries." Also notice in this verse that Paul says we are praying out mysteries <u>with our own spirits</u>, not God's Spirit. How does something we didn't know get into our spirits? That one is easy! By God's Spirit, who is now one with our spirits.

> *For who among men knows a person's thoughts except their own spirit within him? In the same way no one knows the thoughts of God except the Spirit of God.*
>
> —1 Corinthians 2:11

---

18. http://www.dictionary.reference.com/browse/edified

When our spirits pick up on the thoughts of God, our minds also pick up on these thoughts. When our minds pick up on the thoughts of God, we call this "revelation," being "enlightened," or as Paul says, being "edified." Now you know why Paul said he was glad that he prayed in tongues more than anyone else; he received the benefit of knowing the will of God in every situation.

This is what Paul is referring to in 1 Corinthians 2:15-16:

> *The person with the Spirit makes judgments about all things, but such a person is not subject to merely human judgments, for, "Who has known the mind of the Lord so as to instruct him?" But we have the mind of Christ.*

We are not limited to simple human judgment, but we can make judgments about all things. This is great news! We have the ability, by praying in the Spirit (tongues), to receive mysteries, things we did not know; and by that knowledge, we are able to make right judgments about all things!

THE BAPTISM OF THE HOLY SPIRIT IS GOD'S SECRET WEAPON!

The Baptism of the Holy Spirit is God's secret weapon! He can download His will into the earth without the devil knowing what is going on. In fact, praying in the Spirit is listed as part of our spiritual armor in Ephesians 6:18a:

> *And pray in the spirit on all occasions with all kinds of prayers and requests.*

Praying in the Spirit allows us to pick up on strategies that will allow us to sidestep the enemy, or to advance with unique and unusual tactics. Paul says that the Spirit of God will reveal to us those things that have been freely given to us.

The implied benefit is that we can make right decisions in life by tapping into the mind of Christ. I think you would have to agree that this is pretty awesome!

(Some of this chapter was taken from my book *Your Financial Revolution: The Power of Strategy*. For more information on hearing the Holy Spirit, please consider getting a copy.)

CHAPTER 10

THE LAW OF URGENCY

As I sit here at my home, I am looking out the window toward my backwoods. I live on a wonderful piece of Ohio farmland that has slightly rolling hills with beautiful hardwoods. I own over 55 acres, of which about 20 acres are woods, about 10 to 12 acres are a marsh, and the rest of the acres are grass fields.

The only thing missing was a pond. Yes, the marsh always has water in it and makes for some great duck hunting in the fall but, really, is not deep enough for fish to survive the heat of summer. Last year, I decided to put a nice pond in behind the house. If I am sitting on my back deck, I am facing the marsh, the woods, and now, there is a beautiful pond there as well. I am excited about that. The real reason I put the pond in is because I love to fish. I grew up by a pond, and I cannot count all the evenings my friends and I would be sitting out on that pond catching catfish.

When I built the Now Center, our ministry headquarters, I put a pond right behind my back-office door, and my fly rod is right there waiting on me. I keep that pond stocked with big rainbow trout, and I can just slip out my office door, walk about 40 feet, and catch my evening meal. I wanted to have that same option here at home. So, I stocked my new pond with trout, yellow perch, bluegill, and catfish. Wow, what a great setup.

The reason I brought up fishing is because it will serve to

illustrate the law of urgency that is so important to your assignment.

Last week, I taught at several churches in Florida. One of my friends has a house down that way right on the Gulf Coast beach, and he invited me to stay a couple of nights at his house. Well, I was not going to pass that up, especially if I got to fish a bit while I was there. So Drenda and I stayed there a couple of nights. The first morning, I walked out to the beach, and in about an hour, I had caught six whiting, two catfish, one ladyfish, and two sharks. We had the sharks and whiting for lunch.

But here is the lesson. When I am fishing, I am fishing. I stand there with my pole in my hand waiting for the smallest bump. I am always on alert. I am ready to pull on that pole in the twinkling of an eye. Because of that, I do not miss many fish either. It was about two months ago that I had a pole out and was not holding it. Wouldn't you know it? A fish grabbed that line, and that pole went straight up in the air and out into the ocean. I was caught flat-footed and missed that fish and my pole!

So here is the law of urgency: **Do you want to fish or cut bait?**

I am sure you have heard that familiar saying before. It speaks of two people, one who is preoccupied with cutting bait, with a strong emphasis on the word preoccupied, and the other who is focused on fishing. When I am fishing, I am on guard, ready to react at any minute. But I have gone fishing with people who are just so unengaged that they are paying no attention to their line. A fish hits their line, and I have to yell, "Hey, you have a bite!" Then by the time they grab their pole, the fish is gone. Or I have to say, "Hey, it looks like you need some bait on that hook" or "Hey, let me help you get your line out of that tree." I think we can all relate to people like this.

I know it sounds like I am talking about fishing, but I'm not. I am talking about your employees, the people you hang with, and possibly even you. I am talking about missed opportunities. Here is the truth of the matter. People who are distracted do not even know they missed an opportunity! If you hired me as a consultant, and you already did by buying this book, I can guarantee you that you are missing opportunities; and by not engaging this law, you are losing a ton of money.

My wife called a local Honda dealer the other day because we need some repair work done on our ATV. Well, they said it would be three to four weeks before they could get it in there. So, my wife said, "Well, that would be too late. My husband also wants to buy a new ATV while he is there. Is there any way you can get this one in any sooner? We just need to have the battery replaced and some new tires put on. "No. Sorry, not possible." That is a strong statement that it is not possible. Not possible? It would take maybe an hour to do that, probably less. Drenda then told the service manager on the phone, "Well, that's too bad because you will be missing a sale. I guess we will take it over to so and so's Honda shop then, but thanks for your time." The service manager then said, "Okay, sorry." Let me translate my wife's statement to the service manager. "I know we bought the machine from you, but we probably will never come back to your shop again."

Now, let's assume that the service department is just totally maxed out. I mean they are working before hours and after hours servicing everyone's ATVs. How would you have handled the call? I would have checked with everyone there, maybe even offered a small bonus in pay if someone was willing to stay over and take care of this. Anyone with half a brain would realize that they are not just turning down a service call but probably a client who had trusted them before, is now going to the competition, and probably will not be back.

As I thought back on my experience buying my ATV from that dealer in the first place, I remembered the lack of attention they gave me. No one came to help me; I had to find someone to help me. Their explanation of all the ins and outs of the ATV did not happen. In fact, about six months later, I received a package in the mail with the operator's manual for my machine, along with a handwritten note stating, "We found this sitting around in the service department, and we did some checking and found out it was for your machine."

Based on our experience with this service manager, there are a couple of things I can tell you about that guy. First, he is not the owner! And secondly, he probably puts more energy into his bowling league than he does his work. But this guy is not an anomaly in our culture; this is our culture.

Okay, I need to be a little more direct here, and I want to reference a parable that Jesus told in Luke 16. I know, it is a bit long, but you need to really take the time and think about what Jesus is saying here.

> *Jesus told his disciples: "There was a rich man whose manager was accused of wasting his possessions. So he called him in and asked him, 'What is this I hear about you? Give an account of your management, because you cannot be manager any longer.'*
>
> *The manager said to himself, 'What shall I do now? My master is taking away my job. I'm not strong enough to dig, and I'm ashamed to beg—I know what I'll do so that, when I lose my job here, people will welcome me into their houses.'*
>
> *So he called in each one of his master's debtors. He asked the*

first, 'How much do you owe my master?'

'Nine hundred gallons of olive oil,' he replied.

The manager told him, 'Take your bill, sit down quickly, and make it four hundred and fifty.'

Then he asked the second, 'And how much do you owe?'

'A thousand bushels of wheat,' he replied.

He told him, 'Take your bill and make it eight hundred.'

The master commended the dishonest manager because he had acted shrewdly. For the people of this world are more shrewd in dealing with their own kind than are the people of the light. I tell you, use worldly wealth to gain friends for yourselves, so that when it is gone, you will be welcomed into eternal dwellings.

Whoever can be trusted with very little can also be trusted with much, and whoever is dishonest with very little will also be dishonest with much. So if you have not been trustworthy in handling worldly wealth, who will trust you with true riches? And if you have not been trustworthy with someone else's property, who will give you property of your own?

No one can serve two masters. Either you will hate the one and love the other, or you will be devoted to the one and despise the other. You cannot serve both God and money."

—Luke 16:1-13

Wow, Wow, Wow! This parable really just nails the issue on the head. This employee could not have cared less about the owner of the ATV shop. (Excuse me, I am making the parable relevant to our story.) All he cared about was leaving at 5:00 or a myriad of other possibilities. But if he had started that business from scratch, had a clear picture of all that overhead he had to pay out just to run that shop, and he understood that he was the last guy to get paid if there was any money left after payroll, then I can guarantee you he would never have said, "not possible."

In the parable, Jesus is saying this dishonest manager had the ability to think like an owner, but all he thought about was himself. He was a dishonest employee! No, let me rephrase that: He was a dishonest person. He was a hireling.

And if you have not been trustworthy with someone else's property, who will give you property of your own?

He is the guy that is on his phone the whole time he is fishing and wonders how he missed the fish.

It is so amazing to me to have watched this play out in my own business over the years. I have hired graphic and marketing people that just were not urgent. I would have to keep reminding them to post this or to be sure this or that event was on the website. Sometimes I would find an event that happened months ago still on the website. But then I would find out they had their own "on the side" business, and I looked at their website, and it was perfect and beautiful, and the links all worked. Or I had an employee that just seemed to be so slow to get anything done, and then I was shocked to watch them get their personal mandates done with extreme urgency.

Quite frankly, this lack of urgency and lack of ownership have become epidemic in this country. I am sure you can see it at the local fast-food restaurants in your town. We had a McDonald's in our town where the help would stack the chairs on the tables and turn the dining area lights off one hour before they closed. The lights were on up front where the cash registers were, but the seating area's lights were off. Everyone thought they were closed when they pulled up and saw chairs on top of the tables and the lights off.

One day, I walked in when the lights were off and the chairs were on top of the tables, and I said, "Hey, I am sorry. I know you are closing, but I just need to get a tea to go." I was shocked when the cashier said, "Oh, you're good. We do not close for another hour." I asked, "Is your dining room open?" "Sure, just take the chairs off of any table." So, I asked if the dining room was open until closing time, and he replied that it was. "So," I said, "can you tell me why your chairs are on top of the tables and your dining room lights are off every night an hour before you close?" "Oh, you can always come in. The manager likes to leave right at closing time, so he wants the floors mopped and the chairs set up ready to close." "Interesting. So, your manager prepares to close while he is still open instead of preparing to stay open when he is open." Sounds like a hireling to me!

Are you open or not?

Here is a trustworthy statement based on what Jesus taught. Never put a hireling in charge of your stuff—NEVER. I suppose the good thing about this cultural slide into mediocrity is if you show up on time, you stand out like the sun in a dark world. Every employer I know is having trouble finding help that think like owners. Paying heed to this law of acceleration will not only make you some big money but also could cause you to suddenly advance above your peers, straight to the top, just like Joseph did when he was brought up out of that prison and stood before Pharaoh then became the second in command in all of Egypt. There are no small or insignificant positions in life. God knows your heart and your discipline to operate with integrity and

THERE ARE NO SMALL OR INSIGNIFICANT POSITIONS IN LIFE.

urgency. He will be sure people find out about you.

In the introduction, I told you my story of how I discovered the law of urgency as one of the nine laws that I needed to master. As I said in the introduction, besides pastoring a large church and doing daily TV, I also own a financial company helping people get out of debt and helping people who do not want to risk their retirement money with safe investment options where they do not need to worry about losing principal due to market swings.

For a brief review, I had worked with this one vendor for quite a few years. They have an annual convention for their sales reps that qualify. Well, I always qualified for the trips with about $4,000,000 in business a year. At the convention, they also recognized the top 10 reps in the company and rewarded them with a $100,000 bonus and some other nice added benefits. For 14 years, I did about the same volume of business with them, around $4,000,000. This particular year, Drenda and I made it to the convention again with our average production of around $4,000,000. Now, don't get me wrong. The conventions themselves were always very nice, and I was grateful to qualify as one of the 80 or so that were there out of the hundreds who were not.

This particular year as I was sitting there watching the top 10 reps get their recognition and bonus, suddenly, the Lord spoke to me and said, "I want you up there!" I was taken aback by what he said for a minute. "Lord, you know why I am not up there. I am busy pastoring and doing daily TV. These guys that are up there do this day in and day out. I do not have time to do that; I am already maxed out." Then I heard Him say, "I want you up there to be a witness for me." It was already spring, and to qualify for the top 10, you had to do over $10,000,000 in business.

After discussing this with Drenda, we sowed a seed for the

$10,000,000 in volume and called it done. But we had no idea how we were going to pick up our sales to over $10,000,000 in the remaining time we had left in the year when we had been running $4,000,000 for the previous 14 years. Well, we were going to trust in that anointing and trust God to give us a plan.

It was only a few days later that I had a dream, a very simple one. In the dream, God told me what I needed to do to make the top 10. Strangely, it was only three words, but I knew what He meant when I heard them. The words were simply, "Seize the Moment!"

Seize the Moment!

Praying about the dream, I understood what the Lord was showing me. As you know, I am busy, very busy, but the Lord showed me that because I was busy and because my guys were also busy, sometimes we were not as prompt in responding to our incoming calls for information or service as we needed to be. No one was being lazy; everyone was just busy with other clients.

I interrupt this chapter to give you a quiz. Based on what I just said and from what you have learned already in this book, what is your diagnosis? You're right. We had that dreaded disease called capacity cap. And you say it can be terminal if not addressed quickly? And, doctor, what is your prescription? What's that you say? I should take two processes before bedtime with some current data from administration? Okay, just having a bit of fun here, but the issue is not fun. It is real, and yes, it can be terminal for your vision.

Our processes had to change if we were going to move our production from $4,000,000 to over $10,000,000 in less than a year. So I called a meeting and told the guys that I wanted any client or potential client that calls us to get a call back in the first hour, no matter what. I also did the same. One issue that sometimes made very quick follow-up tough was that we have a rule that we must meet with our clients face-to-face if they are investing over $50,000. I figured no one would want to invest their money without having all their questions answered by a real person, the same person that would become their money coach. Okay, in-person meetings are great, but we are licensed in every state, and our clients are all over the place. But our rule still holds. You must have a face-to-face meeting with any client that is thinking about investing over $50,000 unless the client is not open to that and would rather work over Zoom or via a phone call. Otherwise, we were prepared and postured to meet anywhere in the country face-to-face. I realized that God was saying we needed to seize every moment, and that was not going to be easy.

I remember a cruise our family took from New York City to Rome that year, and based on my rule, I was returning calls and setting up appointments in the middle of the Atlantic Ocean. There were many times that I was tired and already maxed out when someone from the West Coast would call me. I would set a 9:30 p.m. appointment with them and fly out there, leaving here in Ohio at 9:00 p.m. (EST), knowing I could just make it there in time for our appointment. Then, I would fly back on a red-eye flight leaving there at midnight their time, 3:00 a.m. my time, get in around 7:00 a.m., get some breakfast, and then go to work. I had to learn to sleep on the plane. Many nights, I did not want to go. I was already tired, but the words "seize the moment" would come back to my mind, and I would head out.

At the end of the year, we made it. We were in the top 10, and we were on the stage and received the $100,000 bonus check. But here is the interesting fact. We made the $10,000,000 goal by one case. One case! If I had backed out of just one of my client calls during that year, we would not have made it. By seizing the moment, every other area of business went up as well.

The next year, that vendor raised the minimum required amount of production to $12,000,000 to qualify for the bonus and be in the top 10. So, Drenda and I sowed our seed and believed God for that $12,000,000; and we made it, again by one case. The next year was the same story and every year after that for the next six years.

I can remember when we did $12,000,000 the first year. The trip for the convention was Budapest. What a glorious city that is! But on that trip, people began to ask me, "How did you do what you did? How much did you spend on marketing? I would answer, "Nothing. We did no marketing; it was all word of mouth." And they just could not believe that. Of course, I always told them about my story and how the Kingdom of God changed my life. Being on that stage gave me a platform to share the Gospel many times.

In the introduction, I left you with a question: "How did we go from doing $4,000,000 to doing over $10,000,000 with that one vendor?" In actuality, the changes we made helped us do more with every other vendor as well, pushing our total investment production close to $20,000,000 in total for the year.

Being intentional and being urgent in every situation completely changed how we did business. A whole new shift in how we operated internally took place. The reality is that the biggest change that took place was how we thought and managed each day. Of course, none of this would have been possible without understanding the law of strategy. I so needed to hear the Holy Spirit for wisdom and creative ideas to reach our goals. It was the Holy Spirit who said that we were operating way below our potential and pointed out what we needed to change to take new territory.

> *Trust in the Lord with all your heart, and lean not on your own understanding; in all your ways* ***acknowledge Him****, and He shall direct your paths.*
>
> —Proverbs 3:5-6 (NKJV)

Think of a large group in a meeting. The chairman of the meeting will say, "I would like to acknowledge the gentleman in the back with the red sweater on." What is he saying? "I invite you to speak. I acknowledge your raised hand." The same is true of the Holy Spirit. Do not lean to your own understanding.

LET HIM SPEAK!

Salespeople are good at talking, and sales meetings are fun, but being urgent is not. Urgency is never convenient. It is always intentional. This is why I said, "Do you want to fish or cut bait?" Sure, there is a time when bait needs to be cut and prepared—but not when the fish are biting. That is the time to be urgent. Urgency demands a clear goal and a clear plan of execution. It is easy to get pulled in different directions when you are busy. That was our error. We needed to stay focused instead of being busy. All of this demanded that we look at our processes; and when we did, we saw that our capacity was capped in many areas. Our salespeople were doing too much paperwork, too many sticky notes were being plastered around and on their desks. Too many of them were having to manage the administration side of their business, and we had to make changes that would free them up to be with their clients.

I am sure that many have helped to bail hay in the summer. The hay has to be put in the barn before it is rained on, because when the hay gets wet, it will mildew and be ruined. There were many times I would get a quick call from my uncle, who bailed a lot of hay, saying he needed my help getting the hay in before the rain started. If rain was approaching, it was everyone on deck. Everyone dropped what they were doing and bailed hay, and we did not stop until all the hay was in the barn.

So here is the question you need to answer. Are you urgently pursuing anything right now, or are you cutting bait? How can you tell? Well, how much time are you spending watching TV, searching on your phone, or wasting time? Secondly, are you pursuing the right things, those things that are going to make the biggest impact in your life? How is your relationship with God, your marriage, your kids? And when you are engaging your harvest field, are you urgently engaged, listening to the Holy Spirit for wisdom, and are quick to move and slow to procrastinate? Are you paying attention to the law of occupancy where you are getting the data from administration, paying close attention to the details so you can be proactive instead of reactive with your decisions?

ARE YOU URGENTLY PURSUING ANYTHING RIGHT NOW, OR ARE YOU CUTTING BAIT?

I was doing an evening conference in Pennsylvania on a Christian TV station. The live event was scheduled to be over at around 10:00 that evening. Now, there was a house that borders my property that had gone into a sheriff's sale that was to be held at 10:00 a.m. the following morning. It was a property that I had been watching for a while, and since it bordered my property, I wanted to buy it. I figured I could use it as a rental or one of my kids might need it as transitional housing sometime. I drove all night long back to Ohio and got home 30 minutes before the sheriff's sale was to start. I got the house. But this is the mindset you must have; harvest demands urgency! Of course, we do not live in a state of urgency, but when the fish are biting, it needs to be all hands on deck.

THIS IS THE MINDSET YOU MUST HAVE; HARVEST DEMANDS URGENCY!

Those three words made me hundreds of thousands of dollars in the last six years.

Seize the Moment!

Just three simple words, but when I applied them, they changed my world; and I am sure they will change yours as well.

The law of urgency.

Chapter 11

THE LAW OF SIGNIFICANCE

The law of significance is a vital law that has the ability to completely transform your life. I am excited to share it with you. If I had to title our discussion today, I would name it:

Going for great and missing significance

When I was in high school, I fell in love with hunting. Typically, rabbits and squirrels were my main quarries. Deer came in the later years of high school, but in the early years, just after I found that old shotgun in middle school, rabbits and squirrels were it. Until one day as I was hunting at a friend's woods, a flock of ducks flew over. They circled, and then I saw them fly to a pond that bordered his property. I had never considered hunting ducks before, but when I saw that flock fly in, I had a sudden urge to consider it. I went home and pulled a few of my hunting magazines out and read a few stories about duck hunting, just looking for some pointers since I had never done that before.

I knew I had to get permission to hunt the pond, and although my friend lived next door to the pond, he did not know who lived there. There was a little white house out toward the road on the property, so one evening, my cousin and I stopped and talked to the folks there. They said they did not own the land but were the caretakers, and they said they didn't care if we hunted there.

There was one thing that all the stories that I had read regarding duck hunting had in them, and that was decoys. So, I went to a sporting goods store and bought six plastic Mallard decoys. The plan was to go hunting the next day after school. Just as we planned, my friend and I drove out to the pond to set our decoys and get ready for the evening hunt. We went about throwing our decoys out and then hid in the grass that bordered the pond and waited. After an hour or so, nothing showed up. But next to the pond, about 200 yards away, was a creek that ran through the property. I had also seen a couple of ducks fly along that creek the day that I saw the flock fly over while I was squirrel hunting. Since there was not much action happening on the pond, my friend and I decided to walk over to the creek to see if any ducks were sitting there. We left the decoys out and walked over to the creek, which had a few large open areas on it that I thought would be good for ducks, but again nothing. So, we decided to go back to the pond and wait out the evening.

As we were walking back toward the pond, we were excited to see a decent sized flock of ducks circle the pond and then land on it. This was perfect. There was an earthen dam all the way around the pond which would keep us hidden as we made our approach and got into position. As I got to the dam and began to crawl up to take a shot, I saw the water covered in ducks. So, I thought I would go ahead and shoot one while they were on the water and then take a second one as the rest lifted off.

Well, as I brought my shotgun up to shoot, the ducks had not seen me yet. I was about to line up on a duck when I saw a larger one that was a little farther out. It was about twice the size of the other ducks. So, I decided to take it. I took aim and fired at the larger duck. At the sound of the gun, the flock lifted off with a roar of wings and quacking. But I was confused, because the larger duck that I had shot at did not take off. Instead, it turned on its side and started to sink. Suddenly, I realized what had happened. I shot my own decoy! I sat there in horror as the decoy slowly sank out of sight. I was more upset about missing the ducks than I was about shooting my own decoy, but I sure felt stupid. My friend came over and asked me if I got one. In embarrassment, I had to admit what I had done. So here is the lesson. It was a great shot, but it was not a significant shot. You can't eat plastic!

Before I begin to dive into this topic, let's define our terms first. The word great, according to definitions.net, means **out of the ordinary** as compared to something else.

The word significance, according to *Collins Dictionary*, means **having a major effect**.

And the word effect, according to the Merriam-Webster Dictionary, means: **the power or ability to produce results: force or influence**.

You can stand out in comparison to others and look great or be great, but are you having a major impact and producing results? For instance, I pulled off a great shot at that plastic decoy but not a significant one because it did not produce the results that I needed or was after.

Let me explain it this way. Let's say I was working on a watch. If I needed a screwdriver, what size screwdriver would I grab? If I grabbed a two-foot long flathead, I could hold it up and say, "Wow, now that is a great screwdriver." But it would have been no good for working on that watch. That big screwdriver had no significance in my situation because it did not have the ability to bring about the results or influence that I needed at that moment. I needed one of those tiny, little screwdrivers to work on a watch. And at that moment, that tiny, little screwdriver, although not great, had great significance because it had the ability to produce the results I needed.

So here are a few questions for you to consider:

- **Do you have a great life or a significant one?**
- **Do you have great employees or significant ones?**
- **Do you have a great career or a significant one?**

Don't go for the decoy!!! Go for significance. It is interesting that most young kids want to be an actor, a singer, or just to become famous. But let's not confuse significance with being great.

I think we can all agree that Jesus was a great leader and led a significant life. So, let's take a quick look at a few lessons we should consider from His life.

> *At sunset, the people brought to Jesus all who had various kinds of sickness, and* ***laying his hands on each one****, he healed them. Moreover, demons came out of many people, shouting, "You are the Son of God!" But he rebuked them and would not allow them to speak, because they knew he was the Messiah.*
>
> *At daybreak, Jesus went out to a solitary place. The people were looking for him and when they came to where he was, they tried to keep him from leaving them. But he said, "I must proclaim the good news of the kingdom of God to the other towns also, because* ***that is why I was sent****."*
>
> —Luke 4:40-43

Jesus had it going on. He was having some **great** meetings, demons were squealing, and people were being healed. It does not get better than that. No wonder the people did not want Him to leave. But Jesus knew significance was better than being great. He could have stayed there and continued to have great meetings, but that was not why He was sent. He knew that He was not there to personally lay hands on every sick person in the world. No, He knew He was there on a much larger mission—to pay the legal price for the sin of all mankind and then to send out an army that would lay **their** hands on the sick and see them healed.

So, what action in that situation would produce the greatest significance for Jesus? We know staying there would have produced some great results, which of course by themselves would have been significant, but which plan would produce the greatest significance? Which plan would produce the results that God had in mind? Okay, let's go a step further. What gave Jesus significance? The same thing that gave that tiny watch screwdriver significance. The ability to produce results and fulfill a purpose.

Purpose!!!!

Without purpose, there is no significance. Oh, people may see the outside, the glitter, but without purpose and results, there is no significance even though there can be greatness. Purpose illuminates and helps us sift the true significance in our lives. Purpose umpires our decisions. Everyone has to answer, "Why was I sent? What is my purpose?"

WITHOUT PURPOSE, THERE IS NO SIGNIFICANCE.

I want to give you what I call nine significance indicators that will help you sift out the deception of greatness and keep you going for significance.

#1 What should you lay your hands on?

As I pointed out in our Scripture, it says that Jesus personally laid His hands on each of the sick people in that meeting. We are all limited with the time we have and need to realize that we cannot lay our hands on everything. We cannot own everything, and we cannot do everything. There are a lot of great ideas and causes out there, all of which are noble with good intent. But are you called to lay your hands there? We do not need more great ideas. We need to find the God idea for our own lives. Jesus did not allow Himself to be distracted from His primary mission. He knew why He was sent and where He needed to lay His hands. He understood the power of significance and wisely used His time to multiply His efforts by duplicating Himself. He sent out the 12 in Mark 6:12, the 72 in Luke 10, and He sent out the church in Mark 16. Now, there are millions of people laying hands on people.

WE DO NOT NEED MORE GREAT IDEAS. WE NEED TO FIND THE GOD IDEA FOR OUR OWN LIVES.

So you need to answer the following question:

What or who are you laying your hands on that will multiply your significance?

Drenda and I have moved several times over our life together. The other day, we went down to our basement and were going through some boxes and came across several boxes that had been packed in Tulsa 25 years ago and never unpacked since then. We were broke back then, and the contents of the boxes we opened were a pitiful display of useless things that we must have thought were precious at the time. Although most of the stuff we opened was nothing but junk, there were a few things that were valuable only as memories. But the crazy thing was that we have moved twice since moving here from Tulsa. That means we just moved those same boxes with us on both of those moves and never opened them to see what we were moving or if we needed it. So how significant were those boxes? Not much if we never even took the time to open them through two complete moves!

What are you carrying that you need to leave behind?

How many times do you lay hands on the same items over and over again? Clear out the junk and detox your life. Here is an assignment for you. Ask yourself the following when you are considering the role something has in your future.

This is a great ___________, but does it add significance (help me have results and influence in relation to my purpose and assignment)? Does it serve my purpose, and DO I NEED IT?

It is not wrong to have a few great things that serve no purpose except for your pleasure, but there is a fine balance in all that. I am sure you have been to homes where they have their collections, shelves and shelves full of stuffed animals, or porcelain animals, or you name it. How does that make you feel when things are stacked all around your home in every square inch of space? Compare that to the feeling you have when you are on vacation and you first arrive at your rented condo or five-star resort room. When you walk into that uncluttered room, it is like taking a breath of fresh air. It is so inviting and free. There is creativity in that order. There is peace for the soul there. Make your office and home that inviting!

I had a couple that came to my church back when we first started. They were newly married. She grew up on a chicken farm, and her family had a routine after every meal. They would put the food scraps in a bowl that they kept on the windowsill to take out to the chickens. Her husband told me that they were in their first month of marriage, and he could not figure out why his new wife kept putting the dinner scraps in a bowl on the windowsill. So, one day he asked her. She then gave the explanation that I just told you. Her husband said to her after her explanation, "But, Honey, we don't have any chickens!" What kind of baggage are you carrying around? Everything you own owns you. Everything you own demands attention. It needs to be oiled, washed, waxed, or stored.

Your vision is too small if you can't declutter!

#2 Who are you? Jesus knew who He was.

What is your uniqueness? Most people do not know who they are. I was in Paris a few years ago in the late fall where you really needed to wear a jacket if you were outside. Drenda and I were walking down a street with very high-end retail stores. We were looking at all the current fashions in the store windows and realized that black was the new black. Everything was black. The streets were crowded that day, and as I looked at all those hundreds of people walking down the street, all I could see was black. Out of literally hundreds of people, not one had a speck of color on. Every person had on black and gray. Everyone wants to be just like everyone else, but it is your uniqueness that makes you valuable to your purpose. Make sure you keep that in mind.

...IT IS YOUR UNIQUENESS THAT MAKES YOU VALUABLE TO YOUR PURPOSE.

#3 Know you need to hear from God.

> *Very early in the morning, while it was still dark, Jesus got up, left the house and went off to* ***a solitary place****, where he prayed.*
>
> —Mark 1:35

Jesus knew He needed to spend time with God and stay focused on His assignment. In the midst of great success, Jesus knew He needed God. It is a huge mistake to trust in yesterday's victories and strategies. There are many reasons why, but let me give you a really big one. You have an adversary who wants to derail your life, or worse, take your life. This is something you must always be aware of on your journey.

> *We do, however, speak a message of wisdom among the mature, but not the wisdom of this age or of the rulers of this age, who are coming to nothing. No, we declare God's wisdom, a mystery that has been hidden and that God destined for our glory before time began. None of the rulers of this age understood it, for if they had, they would not have crucified the Lord of glory.*
>
> —1 Corinthians 2:6-8

Notice it says that if Satan had known the plan of God, he would have changed plans. The plan that worked yesterday may not work today because Satan may have picked up on it and is prepared for it. You always need a fresh revelation from God to fight your battles.

I received an email from one of my partners a while back. He said that when he first started applying Kingdom law in his real estate business, he began to have huge successes. But now, after about six months, he said he has run into all kinds of problems. Problems with his staff, problems closing deals that should have closed, and so on. He was confused. I wrote him back and said, "What are you going to do about it?" A strange reply to an email asking for help, I know. But I wanted to put the ball in his court. He needed to understand that he had now crossed into a new strategy by the enemy but he had the authority to deal with it. I did not leave him with that blunt answer. I went on to explain that he was now on the enemy's radar. His success and his testimony of God's Kingdom had rattled the kingdom of darkness, and they had changed tactics. I encouraged him with this Scripture.

> *Some Jews who went around driving out evil spirits tried to invoke the name of the Lord Jesus over those who were demon-possessed. They would say, "In the name of the Jesus whom Paul preaches, I command you to come out." Seven sons of Sceva, a Jewish chief priest, were doing this. One day the evil spirit answered them, "**Jesus I know, and Paul I know about, but who are you?**" Then the man who had the evil spirit jumped on them and overpowered them all. He gave them such a beating that they ran out of the house naked and bleeding.*
>
> —Acts 19:13-16

I told him I was glad his name was known in hell; it should be. "*But who are you?*" I wanted to make sure, again, that he knew that he had authority to deal with the enemy's tactics of frustration.

The greatest weapon we have is what I have already shared in the law of strategy chapter, the Holy Spirit. Let's go to a very familiar Bible story, and I will explain.

> *As the Philistine moved closer to attack him, David ran quickly toward the battle line to meet him. Reaching into his bag and taking out a stone, he slung it and struck the Philistine on the forehead. The stone sank into his forehead, and he fell facedown on the ground.*
>
> *So David triumphed over the Philistine with a sling and a stone; without a sword in his hand he struck down the Philistine and killed him.*
>
> —1 Samuel 17:48-50

In this well-known Bible story, David is confronting Goliath, a giant of a man and a trained warrior from his youth. To put it bluntly, David did not stand a chance, or did he? David tried on the armor of King Saul, and it did not fit him. Again, David would not have stood a chance if he had attempted to defeat Goliath with strategy that Goliath was expecting. Instead, David leaned to a completely different strategy, one that no one expected and one that took Goliath completely by surprise.

> *He said to David, "Am I a dog, that you come at me with sticks?"*
>
> —1 Samuel 17:43a

David held his staff in one hand and a sling in the other. I am sure that David hid his sling as he approached Goliath and was using his staff as a decoy. Goliath was confused. Here was this kid with no sword, armed with only a stick, coming against him? But David had his plan. Instead of walking into battle, the Bible says that David ran toward Goliath. I am sure that was part of the surprise factor that David was counting on. Running toward Goliath would make it more difficult for Goliath to have time to discern the real danger, which was the sling. So, what was David's real weapon? A supernatural strategy by the Holy Spirit.

This is why I am telling you that you need to spend time with God. Even in the midst of success, the enemy will always try to interfere with God's plans. There is no fear in that, and do not let the enemy tempt you to fear. He has been defeated and holds no power or authority over you.

My partner I told you about adjusted a few things in his office and his company structure, and today is prospering at an even greater level than he ever has.

LET GOD SHOW YOU WHAT YOU NEED TO DO. NEVER GO IT ALONE; ALWAYS MAKE SURE YOU TAKE THE TIME TO HEAR.

Let God show you what you need to do. Never go it alone; always make sure you take the time to hear.

#3 Does this relationship bring significance to my life?

God uses people, and so does Satan. Be careful of your relationships. Learn to say no, and learn to protect your time. Do not allow yourself to become someone's answer. Always point them to Jesus. I am not saying that you are not to be there for people, but you need to watch for people who are not meeting you halfway and are constantly pulling on you. The enemy loves to use people to wear you out.

When we were young pastors, we felt we needed to be there for people whenever and wherever they needed help. We endured hours and hours of individual meetings. We took false responsibility and would pay their bills for them. Our hearts were right, but without realizing it, the enemy was using these people to wear us out until we despaired of even being in the ministry. There were the marathon phone calls from the same people over and over again that just sucked the life out of us. In our immaturity, we thought we had to fix everyone's problems. But eventually, the Lord showed us to stop that—not that we could not help people, but we had to put the ball into their court.

One wise pastor told us that we did not owe people our time or our money. But we did owe them good, sound instruction for their lives. He reminded us that we were not there to be their close friends but their pastors. He said all we really owed them was to be an example, teach them the Kingdom, and have fun doing it. He said if we were not having fun, then why would anyone else want to serve God? We had to agree, and we made changes in how we managed our time and how we held people accountable.

#4 What are you doing?

I must ________________. They tried to keep Jesus from leaving their town, "*But He said, I must proclaim the good news of the kingdom of God to the other towns also, because that is why I was sent*" (Luke 4:43).

Doing great things is no replacement for doing significant things. What should you be doing today that you are not doing, or what are you doing today that you should not be doing?

You can only say no when you know your yes!

#5 Where should you be doing it? Where is your territory, your niche, or assignment?

Notice that Jesus knew He had to go to the other towns and that was why He was sent. Jesus could judge His progress because He knew where He was going.

Let me say that again. You can only judge your progress when you know where you are going. This goes back to our previous four laws, but if you do not know where you are going, how will you know when you get there or if you ever will get there?

#6 That was the reason I was sent.

What is your reason, your cause, your crusade? Making money is a horrible cause. The minute you have some, you will stop. No, you must have a clear purpose that is bigger than money! Only having a personal crusade will get you up in the morning. No one has to tell Drenda and me to show up at church, to preach, or to tell someone about the Kingdom. It is not our job. It is who we are. When what you do becomes your hobby, then you are on the right track.

#7 Who do you want to tell? And what do you want to tell them?

The key word here is want. Who are you drawn to? What assignment or mission excites you? Your significance is always answered with that question. When your have to becomes your get to, you are headed in the right direction. Of course, every assignment has things in it that we may not enjoy. But the overall filter is that you are drawn to the assignment, you have passion for it. Walking in the assignment actually energizes you, and you are excited about your future.

Your future must be bigger than your today or you might quit in a time of pressure.

#8 Live like you do one week before vacation.

You know how you make that huge to-do list right before you go on vacation? How you get up early and stay up late? You are intense and focused. It is amazing how many things you get done that week. The reward set before you, your vacation, motivates you to work at a different level of intensity. Find the purpose for your life that causes you to live like that every day.

#9 Don't Quit!

I think this one speaks for itself. Quitting is not an option. If you really feel like quitting, stop and take a vacation. It is always easier to see clearly when you are rested.

Finally, remember you are here not to be great but significant. In being significant, you will become great!

CHAPTER 12

THE LAW OF GENEROSITY[19]

Our family was eating dinner one night at one of our favorite local restaurants. The waitress was a young lady who was very pregnant. As I was about to pay our bill, I suddenly felt led to give her a big tip instead of the 22 to 25% I usually give, so I added $100 to the tip amount. She picked up the signed Visa slip without looking at it and walked back toward the kitchen. In a minute she was back, with tears streaming down her face. She came back to thank us. She told us how she was in a tight financial situation and was wondering how she could make it. We had the opportunity to share Christ with her and pray for her before we left. We did nothing but be generous to open the door of ministry to her heart.

> *Or do you show contempt for the riches of his kindness, forbearance and patience, not realizing that God's kindness is intended* ***to lead you to repentance****?*
>
> —Romans 2:4

The New King James Version says that God's goodness leads us to repentance.

Being generous is acting like God does.

---

19. Excerpt taken from my book *Your Financial Revolution: The Power of Generosity*

> *That you may be children of your Father in heaven. He causes his sun to rise on the evil and the good and sends rain on the righteous and the unrighteous.*
>
> —Matthew 5:45

God is good, and He is generous! We are His children, and our new nature in Christ is one of being generous as well. As in the story above, being generous is sharing God's heart for people. Like taking a sip of cold water on a very hot day, being generous brings relief and hope to a world that is in the desert of poverty. The impact of giving freely is clearly seen in Paul's instruction to the church in Corinth.

> *Now he who supplies seed to the sower and bread for food will also supply and increase your store of seed and will enlarge the harvest of your righteousness. You will be enriched in every way so that you can be generous on every occasion, and through us your generosity will result in thanksgiving to God.*
>
> *This service that you perform is not only supplying the needs of the Lord's people but is also overflowing in many expressions of thanks to God. Because of the service by which you have proved yourselves, others will praise God for the obedience that accompanies your confession of the gospel of Christ, and for your generosity in sharing with them and with everyone else. And in their prayers for you their hearts will go out to you, because of the surpassing grace God has given you. Thanks be to God for his indescribable gift!*
>
> —2 Corinthians 9:10-15

Your generosity causes people to praise and thank God!!!

Notice that Paul says that being generous is your service to God. The definition of the word service is: The performance of work or duties for a superior or as a servant.[20] It is part of your duty on God's behalf here in the earth realm to share His heart and concern for people. The result is clear—it touches people's hearts and opens them to receive Christ. I think we can all remember when someone came to our aid and how much it meant to us.

Generosity shows people your and God's heart for them!

Generosity is so powerful. It supersedes words and goes straight to the heart. It's amazing how we can remember a compliment or a gift that someone gave us. There are times that God uses people that we do not even know to encourage us and reach out to us.

GENEROSITY IS SO POWERFUL. IT SUPERSEDES WORDS AND GOES STRAIGHT TO THE HEART.

A time that was especially memorable was the time that Drenda and I went pheasant hunting with some friends. Drenda and I had just gotten married and were living in Tulsa. We drove to Kansas and had a great day of hunting. But on the way back to Tulsa, our friend's car blew its engine. We were in the middle of nowhere on a dirt road and still hours from home. If you have ever been to Kansas, then you know how barren it is. It was dark then, and we only saw one light off in the distance. We hiked to the farmer's home and told him of our situation. I was totally shocked when he said, "Well, I will drive you home tonight. I will put your car on my trailer, and I will get you home in time for work on Monday." Drenda was to start a new job in the morning working part time at a restaurant,

20. https://www.thefreedictionary.com/service

and she was so disappointed that she may have to call in that she would be unable to be there.

Amazingly, this man who we had never met before, drove us five hours home to Tulsa and then drove all the way back home before morning. I will never forget that selfless act of kindness. He would not even take a penny for the gas. I will always be grateful to that man. When I think of him, I always think of his gift with gratitude.

When people think of you, they are going to thank God for your generosity.

One of the most powerful principles I learned is found in the following passage as Paul continues his instruction on giving.

> *This service that you perform is not only supplying the needs of the Lord's people but is also overflowing in many expressions of thanks to God. Because of the service by which you have proved yourselves, others will praise God for the obedience that accompanies your confession of the gospel of Christ, and for your generosity in sharing with them and with everyone else. And in their prayers for you their hearts will go out to you, because of the surpassing grace God has given you. Thanks be to God for his indescribable gift!*
>
> —2 Corinthians 9:12-15

Surpassing means: of a large amount or high degree; exceeding, excelling, or extraordinary: *structures of surpassing magnificence*.[21]

What is going to be yours in a huge amount? What is going to be extraordinary and surpasses magnificence in your life? God's grace!!!!! Let's take a look at the definition of grace.

21. https://www.dictionary.com/browse/surpassing

Grace: God's unmerited favor

This is the standard definition of grace, but let me give you a further definition.

"Common Christian teaching is that grace is unmerited mercy (favor) that God gave to humanity by sending His Son to die on a cross, thus delivering eternal salvation."[22]

However, this definition alone may not cover all uses of the term in Scripture. For example, Luke 2:40 (KJV) says, "*And the child grew, and waxed strong in spirit, filled with wisdom: and the grace of God was upon him.*" In this example, when using the definition of grace to mean unmerited favor, it does not make sense that the sinless Christ would need this.

James Ryle has suggested "Grace is the empowering Presence of God enabling you to be who He created you to be, and to do what He has called you to do." Alternatively, Bill Gothard has suggested "Grace gives us the desire and the power that God gives us to do His will." Both of these definitions make good sense of the word grace throughout the Bible.[23]

So we see that what Paul is talking about in this passage is the grace, or the empowerment to prosper! This gift, the gift of grace, was celebrated because it met the people's need. Paul ends his discussion (in 2 Corinthians above) with, "***Thanks be to God for his indescribable gift!***"

Here is the power that can set you free from financial bondage—the grace of God. This power to prosper is available to every believer. But here is the issue. We can spend a lot of time talking about what Paul said to do—to give. But if we do not understand the grace, the empowerment to prosper by the power of God, we miss the harvest of what is needed. It would

22. http://en.wikipedia.org/wiki/divine_grace

23. http://en.wikipedia.org/wiki/divine_grace

be like planting your garden in the woods under the shade of a big tree—there would be no sunshine, no power to bring forth the desired result.

Drenda and I would read stories in the Bible where the power of God showed up and completely changed the situation for the good. I will have to admit that we heard very few such stories occurring in our church as we grew up. Outside of salvation, no one really ever talked about how to bring the grace of God into a situation. Now, I understand that our salvation is the most important thing. But as I just mentioned, I need that same grace to function in every area of my life. But I did not know how. And because of my ignorance, we were broke, sick, and depressed. We knew of salvation—we had the eternal salvation part down—but we did not know or understand how to bring heaven into our lives and manifest the power of God.

This is what the Lord was telling me that day when He spoke to me concerning the Kingdom: "You are in this mess because you have never learned how my Kingdom operates!" In other words, He was saying that I did not know how to release the authority of the King here in the earth realm. I had never learned how or even that I could. Let me make this point here: You will never be free until you are financially free.

And as Drenda and I have been saying for years, you will never discover your spiritual purpose until you fix the money thing. And let me make this point also—YOU CAN GET FREE! You must get financially free not only for yourself but also so people can see the Kingdom of God operating; and like a fruit tree laden with ripe fruit, it will attract people to it. People are looking for answers; they are looking for the real deal. They desperately need to see the Kingdom and not religion.

One example sticks out to me and illustrates how a lot of America lives. A lady called me to visit her as she needed help with her debt. I and one of my associates met with her, and I sat there in unbelief as she explained her situation. She had 32 different credit cards, all maxed out. She had successfully built her own prison, and she was asking me for the key to get out. In my mind, the answer was easy: *Stop using credit cards; that would be a good start.* So I told her to cut up the cards and insisted that she live within her income. I also suggested she start using a debit card. She instantly burst into tears and made this shocking statement. "How will I be able to buy shoes?" Did I hear that right? She did not have enough money for food, but she was asking about shoes?

You may think that she must be an anomaly; and in the number of cards, she was. But in being in financial prison, she was not. Look at the latest stats in America.

- 56% of people do not have $1,000 in the bank.[24]
- 40% cannot pay an unexpected $400 bill.[25]

Friend, America is just as God told me; people are slaves. Think of what a slave does. He does not work for himself. Although he (or she) is working and producing profit, the profit is sent to lenders each month, leaving just enough for the family to survive another month. A slave lives in a house they do not own (meaning they have a mortgage) and drive cars they do not own to pay for the house they do not own. They wear clothes they bought on their

24. Carmen Reinicke, "56% of Americans Can't Cover a $1,000 Emergency Expense with Savings," www.cnbc.com, January 19, 2022

25. Soo Youn, "40% of Americans Don't Have $400 in the Bank for Emergency Expenses: Federal Reserve," www.abc.go.com, May 24, 2019

Visa card to go to work, to pay for their car and the house they do not own, along with the student loan they are still paying off. You get the idea.

> *The rich rule over the poor, and the borrower is slave to the lender.*
>
> —Proverbs 22:7

As I mentioned previously, over 80% of people do not like their jobs, and 33% actually hate their jobs.[26] Why then do they work where they work? Because they are slaves, and slaves do not have options! So, is there a way out of slavery? Yes! Don't believe me? Let me show you.

> *This service that you perform is not only supplying the needs of the Lord's people but is also overflowing in many expressions of thanks to God. Because of the service by which you have proved yourselves, others will praise God for the obedience that accompanies your confession of the gospel of Christ, and for your generosity in sharing with them and with everyone else. And in their prayers for you their hearts will go out to you, because of the surpassing grace God has given you. Thanks be to God for his indescribable gift!*
>
> —2 Corinthians 9:12-15

Let's stay focused on that answer, the grace of God. The empowerment to prosper!

Let's also be aware that the enemy wants you to stay in debt and never learn of the way out. That is why there are 1.2 billion

26. Ken Keis, Ph.D., "Why Do People Hate Their Jobs?" Linkedin.com, October 6, 2014

active credit cards in the US. It is also the reason 7 to 8 billion credit card offers are sent out every year.[27] Someone wants you in debt, and it is not just the banks and retailers who are begging you to try their cards. Satan knows if he can keep you in debt, you will never be able to walk in your spiritual destiny—which he knows would wreak havoc in his kingdom.

So, let me review for a minute. This chapter is about being generous, right? Well, yes and no. Yes, we are going to talk about all the benefits of giving and being generous in a bit. But giving by itself is not the answer without having the knowledge of how to tap into the grace, the power of God. So, let me state again: The formula of giving by itself, just as a formula, is not the key. It is part of it, of course, but you and I need that supernatural, extraordinary empowerment to prosper called grace.

Dustin and Kendall discovered what I am talking about. They are a young couple who did not really understand they needed the grace of God in their finances until they found themselves in a mess. They had just looked at a new business idea and decided to move on it. The cost? $150,000, all of it debt. The same month they bought the business, they were audited by the IRS and were billed for $53,000 in back taxes. Dustin said they found themselves over $200,000 in debt with really no way out, especially since things were already tight financially before they bought the business. They had just borrowed the money to pay the hospital for their last baby and were making payments on that. The audit pushed them over the financial edge, and Dustin scrambled to find options.

After searching, he finally found an offer for a $30,000 line of credit, was approved, and took this idea to his wife for her opinion.

27. Bianca Peter, "Number of Credit Cards and Credit Card Holders," https://www.wallethub.com, July 15, 2020

What he did not know was that his wife, Kendall, had been studying and meditating on my book *Your Financial Revolution: The Power of Rest*, which also talks about tapping into the grace of God. So when Dustin came to her with this loan idea, she was disappointed, hoping he would turn to God instead. She decided to talk to him about their decision and encouraged him to trust God. Graciously, he received the wisdom of his wife. As they prayed, they heard the Holy Spirit say to sow a seed. Of course, at the time, they did not have the money for the amount that God had shown them to give, so they worked for the next 28 days to earn enough to sow what God had shown them. The result? Their business took off.

Over the next year, they were able to pay off $175,000 in debt, and Dustin said he made 12 times more money that year than he had ever made in his entire life. Kendall and Dustin found out the Kingdom works every time!

The answer: Grace

We have been talking about how generosity impacts people spiritually, how it softens their hearts with gratitude toward you and God. We also brought out what Paul said, that this ability to be generous is a result of the grace of God in our lives.

> *And in their prayers for you their hearts will go out to you, because of the surpassing grace God has given you. Thanks be to God for his indescribable gift!*
>
> —2 Corinthians 9:14-15

We talked about the emphasis Paul put on the word surpassing when he described the grace that God has given us to prosper. We found out that grace means an extraordinary empowerment to accomplish something. Paul calls this empowerment of God's grace to help us prosper an indescribable gift! I think anyone would have to admit that if God Himself was going to help them prosper in life, they would prosper. To help you grasp the magnitude of what God wants to do in your life and the immense power available to you, let's back up a few verses and begin to read at verse six.

> *This is what I mean: The one who sows sparingly will also reap sparingly. The one who sows generously will also reap generously. Each one should give as he has determined in his heart, not reluctantly or under pressure, for God loves a cheerful giver.*
>
> *God is able to make all grace overflow to you, so that in all things, at all times, having all that you need, you will overflow in every good work. As it is written: "He scattered; he gave to the poor. His righteousness remains forever."*
>
> *And he who provides seed to the sower and bread for food will provide and multiply your seed for sowing, and will increase the harvest of your righteousness. You will be made rich in every way so that you may be generous in every way, which produces thanksgiving to God through us.*
>
> —2 Corinthians 9:6-11 (EHV)

Now, here is where things get really exciting! We see that same word grace used here except in this passage Paul adds the term "all" to the word grace. Paul is clearly talking about giving and receiving here and makes the point that once you give, all of God's grace is available to bring in the harvest. All of God's grace simply implies that all of God's power, His wisdom, favor, and insight are now available to you to capture the harvest on that seed. I do not know about you, but that gets me excited. But that still does not mean the harvest is just going to happen all by itself.

If a very wealthy farmer told you that he was going to lend you all of his farming equipment worth millions of dollars to plant and harvest a crop and you knew nothing about farming, it would not profit you a thing. God has made all of His power available to us, but we still have our parts to play. Just as a farmer knows, there is a lot more to farming than just throwing seed into the ground. For now, all I want you to understand at this point is that all of God's ability is standing by to help you harvest after you sow, and secondly, because of that, you have an unlimited future!!!!

...GOD'S ABILITY IS STANDING BY TO HELP YOU HARVEST AFTER YOU SOW, AND SECONDLY, BECAUSE OF THAT, YOU HAVE AN UNLIMITED FUTURE!

So now, let's go a step further and talk about the clear revelation in this passage as to the purpose of having money.

> *God is able to make all grace overflow to you, so that in all things, at all times, having all that you need, you will overflow in every good work.*

We see the first thing God mentions is having all that you need. Notice it is not just money either. He says in all things and at all times! I always say it this way, "You take care of God's business, and He will take care of yours." So, in all things and at all times! This would mean to me that you would never go without, no matter what is happening in the economy. When God says your needs will be met, He is not talking about just getting by either.

> *You will lend to many nations but will borrow from none. The Lord will make you the head, not the tail. If you pay attention to the commands of the Lord your God that I give you this day and carefully follow them, you will always be at the top, never at the bottom.*
>
> —Deuteronomy 28:12b-13

When God is talking about all your needs being met, He is talking about walking in a place of total financial freedom with no debt, walking in your assignment with passion, and eating the best of the land. It also means you are in perfect health and perfect peace.

Secondly, after your needs are met and you are not just surviving,

> *You will be made rich in every way so that you may be generous in every way, which produces thanksgiving to God through us.*

The end result is to move people's hearts toward God. This could mean personally giving to someone in need or giving to a God assignment in the earth realm. Both of these examples are to move people's hearts toward God. With that in mind, let me address a false assumption that I hear so often. Someone once told me that they did not need more money, that they had enough. Well, they missed the entire point of having money in the first place. If you are simply talking about you being comfortable and having everything you need, then I guess there is a place where the drive to obtain more money could diminish. But here is the part that you really need to grab ahold of. God needs more money!!!! Let me say that again:

GOD NEEDS MORE MONEY!

There is still a lot of work to be done.

> *God is able to make all grace overflow to you, so that in all things, at all times, having all that you need, you will overflow in every good work.*

You have every good work to attend to. Every good work is work done on behalf of the King. In fact, you have very specific work to do according to Ephesians 4.

> *But to each one of us grace has been given as Christ apportioned it.*
>
> —Ephesians 4:7

> *So Christ himself gave the apostles, the prophets, the evangelists, the pastors and teachers, to equip his people for works of service.*
>
> —Ephesians 4:11-12a

You see, most people aim at being financially free because they are tired of the rat race. They are looking for peace. Since most work in jobs they really do not like, they are looking for the freedom that having money will give them to do what they want to do instead of what they have to do.

Here is a statement that drives the religious people crazy:

> *You will be made rich in every way.*
>
> —2 Corinthians 9:11 (EHV)

Yes, it does say that—you will be made rich! Now, the term rich is subjective and mostly realigned in our culture. We really cannot say that someone who has one billion dollars is any happier than someone with $100,000.

No, being rich is, of course, having all my needs met, eating the best of the land, but it is also playing with my grandkids, holding hands with my wife, and so many other wonderful things in life. Drenda and I have five great kids; all love God and in some way or another are involved in ministry. We all live close to each other, and, quite frankly, we love hanging out with each other. I call that rich!

You see, the religious folks think that having a lot of money is greed. But you cannot have too much money if you are in the people business with God. There is always a new assignment and new territory to take.

YOU CANNOT HAVE TOO MUCH MONEY IF YOU ARE IN THE PEOPLE BUSINESS WITH GOD.

So again, God wants you to have plenty of provision to carry on His work in the world. God wants you to be generous for Him, helping people and funding His assignments. Stop everything! If you are going to be able to be generous on every occasion, you must have some money. I mean, every occasion could be every day or multiple times a day. Let's be honest. To do that, you would not be living month to month. You would have more money than what was needed to pay your bills, a lot more! I think everyone would agree with that. But let's get down to where the rubber meets the road.

What is the fear in giving? That we will not have enough for ourselves, right? *Hey, I need that money*, you may think, and of course you need it. But guess what? As I said, God needs it also. So where is God going to get the money He needs to fund His agenda? That money is going to come from you and me and other fellow believers, of course. Satan's people are not going to fund God's assignments. God is not going to ask you to give Him your money to use without a promise back to you, a return on your investment so to speak, is He? Well, it depends on who you ask.

The majority of believers would say it is wrong to believe God for a return on your giving. They believe giving to God and expecting anything back would be based on greed and diminish the pure act of worshiping God. Do you believe a farmer is off base to believe his sowing will produce a profit for him and his family? Of course not. He is simply using the laws that God gave him. God delights in seeing us prosper. He gave us the law of sowing and reaping for our benefit. Jesus told a parable that addressed this issue. It is a story that has been told in every Sunday school classroom since time began. But for some reason, the teachers always seem to leave an extremely important part of the story out. Let's go to Luke 10 and the parable of the Good Samaritan.

> *On one occasion an expert in the law stood up to test Jesus. "Teacher," he asked, "what must I do to inherit eternal life?"*
>
> *"What is written in the Law?" he replied. "How do you read it?"*
>
> *He answered, "Love the Lord your God with all your heart and with all your soul and with all your strength and with all your mind"; and, "Love your neighbor as yourself."*
>
> *"You have answered correctly," Jesus replied. "Do this and you will live."*
>
> *But he wanted to justify himself, so he asked Jesus, "And who is my neighbor?"*

In reply Jesus said: "A man was going down from Jerusalem to Jericho, when he was attacked by robbers. They stripped him of his clothes, beat him and went away, leaving him half dead. A priest happened to be going down the same road, and when he saw the man, he passed by on the other side. So too, a Levite, when he came to the place and saw him, passed by on the other side.

But a Samaritan, as he traveled, came where the man was; and when he saw him, he took pity on him. He went to him and bandaged his wounds, pouring on oil and wine. Then he put the man on his own donkey, brought him to an inn and took care of him. The next day he took out two denarii and gave them to the innkeeper. 'Look after him,' he said, 'and when I return, I will reimburse you for any extra expense you may have.'

"Which of these three do you think was a neighbor to the man who fell into the hands of robbers?"

The expert in the law replied, "The one who had mercy on him."

Jesus told him, "Go and do likewise."

—Luke 10:25-37

I think all of us have heard this story with the lesson being, "What would God do if He were walking down the road and saw this guy?" We know He would not leave him there to die along the road. The lesson that most Sunday school classes teach from this is taking care of people is God's heart, and I can say I agree one hundred percent. To truly understand Jesus's rebuke, however, you need to know that the Jews despised the Samaritans and considered them unclean. Thus, the Jews viewed themselves as much more holy and righteous in God's eyes than the Samaritans.

So Jesus's story is basically rebuking this teacher of the law for his pious attitude. But the part I never hear, and I mean never, is the part of the story involving the two silver coins.

> *Then he put the man on his own donkey, brought him to an inn and took care of him. The next day he took out two denarii and gave them to the innkeeper. "Look after him," he said, "and when I return, I will reimburse you for any extra expense you may have."*
>
> —Luke 10:34b-35

In the analogy Jesus is teaching, we can see mankind battered and bruised by Satan, the thief. We understand the oil and wine are prophetically representing the Holy Spirit and the blood covenant which Jesus will give to all who come to Him. Jesus goes a step further in the story after applying the oil and wine. He knows the man needs time to heal, and he takes him to a safe place to recover, the inn, all at his expense. The inn represents the local church. This is where Jesus brings the people who have been found battered and dying along life's road. They are born again, having been cleansed from sin by the blood covenant and made alive by the Holy Spirit, yet they still carry with them the stain of the earth curse system. They need time to heal and to learn a completely new way of living. Jesus sets them in a local church and under an innkeeper, the local pastor, to oversee their progress.

But we find the same attitude in the church that the teacher of the law had. People do not want to get involved in helping out at the inn. Pastors spend much of their time begging people to help out in the nursery or to help lead a small group. But it seems people are already busy doing their own thing and find it hard to commit to help. Since people do not commit voluntarily, religion tries to guilt people into helping by saying, "You owe it to God to take care of this or that. After all, look what God has done for you." And I agree, we should always have willing and grateful hearts toward God and have a desire to help others. But God does not operate with the "you owe me system."

He says, "I am leaving you two coins to cover expenses and will pay you WHATEVER it costs you when I return." Now, when he says, "When I return," he is not talking about when Jesus returns but, rather, when the businessman comes back by the inn. There is a parallel prophetically. This statement was meant to imply real-time financial help for that innkeeper.

Now, we may say, "Great. God is going to cover the expense of taking care of this person"; yet that fails to motivate many people, and here is why. If I asked you to feed 200 people for me and I told you that I would cover the cost of the food, you may or may not be excited about doing it. Yes, you could do it out of loyalty to me or duty toward God, and that is required sometimes. But as a lifestyle, if I asked you to do that on a consistent basis, you would probably not be too excited about it.

I believe the reason so many pastors feel like they have to beg their people to get involved is because they have not taught them that God gives a return on our generosity. He wants you to know this is a family business and you have the right to reap from it. Paul talks about this in his letter to the church in Corinth.

> *Who serves as a soldier at his own expense? Who plants a vineyard and does not eat its grapes? Who tends a flock and does not drink the milk? Do I say this merely on human authority? Doesn't the Law say the same thing? For it is written in the*

> *Law of Moses: "Do not muzzle an ox while it is treading out the grain." Is it about oxen that God is concerned? Surely he says this for us, doesn't he? Yes, this was written for us, because whoever plows and threshes should be able to do so in the hope of sharing in the harvest.*
>
> —1 Corinthians 9:7-10

You would have to agree that if you were working in your own business, knowing that you had the right to reap from your efforts, you would be much more motivated and full of passion. This is what God wants you to understand: It is a family business. God does not want you to serve Him out of fear. This would be the duty minded person. He wants it to come from your heart for Him and the joy of the reward.

Jesus chose an innkeeper for the story for a very important reason. We understand that the innkeeper is operating a business. He has built into his daily rate the price for overhead and staff. But on top of all the expenses needed to run the inn, he adds profit. That's right, profit. Every time he charges his guest for a night's stay, he makes a profit. Because of this, the innkeeper has a very different perspective toward the injured man. It is not costing him a cent to take care of him. In fact, the innkeeper understands that each night the man stays there, he will make a profit; and with an open checkbook offered by the traveling businessman, he is probably ecstatic. I can just imagine the innkeeper's conversation with the traveling businessman as he leaves on his journey, "Hey, if you see anyone else who needs help along the road, be sure to bring them here. I will take all you can bring me; and if I run out of room, I will add on!"

As you can see, there is a whole lot more to the story than

just the familiar story of what Jesus would do. Jesus was trying to correct the religious mindset that the expert in the law had toward God and was also making a point that it does not cost to actually care for people. In fact, there is reward with it.

I am always sad when I hear people say that God does bad things to good people or I see people serving God out of a religious duty instead of the exciting life they could have. Satan has tried to hide God's goodness from God's people so that they would not willingly serve Him with their whole hearts. To most, church is an event on the calendar instead of understanding that they are the church, the inn where God sends people to become whole. They sadly miss God's heart—that He is willing to pay whatever it costs to reach people—and He always gives us more than we invest. Always.

SATAN HAS TRIED TO HIDE GOD'S GOODNESS FROM GOD'S PEOPLE SO THAT THEY WOULD NOT WILLINGLY SERVE HIM WITH THEIR WHOLE HEARTS.

I can remember sitting down with Drenda's brother years ago and discussing this very point—that God is good and a rewarder, and He has given us the Kingdom that meets all our needs. This understanding of the Kingdom was new to Johnny and his wife, Candi, as they had come out of a traditional church. Johnny and Candi were teachers in Georgia.

While teaching, Johnny worked part time with my financial company, Forward Financial Group. In his first year with the company, he made more part time than he did the whole year of teaching, so he decided to quit teaching and go full time.

At first, Johnny did very well, but later in that year, I saw that his activity began to slow. I knew that he could not continue at that pace for long. Drenda and I had planned a trip to Georgia for the Christmas season, and I had full intentions of stopping and spending some time with Johnny to see if I could identify some of the reasons that he was not producing the business he needed to stay full time. Before I could call Johnny, he called me and asked if I could stop over to discuss business. Of course, I was already prepared to do just that. I could tell that Johnny and Candi were scared. They already had $5,000 worth of bills due for the current month, and they had no money set to come in for the next month's $5,000 they would need.

As I sat down with Johnny, his first words were, "It is just not working." I knew that the Kingdom understanding was all new to Johnny and Candi, and I felt that I needed to coach them on how to handle this spiritually. Because I knew the Kingdom always works! So I spent about two hours with them going over the laws of the Kingdom and how to release their faith. As I spoke, I could sense fear fading and faith beginning to rise.

I knew Johnny was ready for the next step. "Johnny," I said, "you need to plant a seed with God and believe Him for the money you need." Johnny and Candi agreed, but they had no money. It just so happened that I had brought with me a paycheck for Johnny from the home office totaling $160. I knew they could use that money, and I encouraged them to sow it as a seed as we both knew that the $160, by itself, could not take care of the $5,000 in bills they needed to catch up. They agreed.

As we were about to pray and release our faith together, I asked Johnny, "What are you believing to receive as you sow this money?" As the words left my mouth, the Holy Spirit stopped me and said not to let him answer, and I knew why. Johnny would have said, "I am believing for the $5,000," obviously, as that was where the pressure was. Instead, the Holy Spirit said to me, "Ask him if $12,000 in 30 days would be enough?" So, I did just that. I stopped him from answering and asked him if $12,000 in 30 days would be enough. I could see his eyes open wide as I stated the amount the Lord told me to ask him. I knew that Johnny had never made $12,000 in 30 days in his entire life. He sat there for a minute and then said yes, he could believe that with me. I asked Candi the same question, and she said yes as well. So we joined hands, laid them on that check, and released our faith for $12,000 in 30 days.

Three weeks later, I received a call from Johnny. Boy, was he excited. He had written enough business in the past three weeks to pay him not $12,000 but $17,000. He really was a believer then.

Unfortunately, two months later, Johnny lost control of his car on a rainy night heading home after an appointment. The car was totaled, but Johnny lived through the crash, which in itself was an act of God. However, due to the accident, Johnny was unable to work as he recovered. During that time period, his house fell into foreclosure and was set for a sheriff's sale. He needed $10,000 to pull the house out of the sale.

During this time, however, Johnny and Candi had decided that they needed to move to Ohio to get closer to the Kingdom teaching that was changing their lives. So, they listed the house even though they knew they only had about one month before the sheriff's sale was to occur. As the date drew closer, no real buyers came by until just a few days before the sheriff's sale when a man stopped by and offered to buy the house. But he had a request. He wanted to know if he gave Johnny $10,000 then, could he hold the house for 30 days until he finished up some other business which was going to fund the purchase. Johnny was shocked. He knew that if he was going to pull the house out of the sheriff's sale, it had to be a cash buyer as the sale was only a couple of days away. This buyer wanted to write Johnny a $10,000 check on the spot and then close later. This was the exact amount that Johnny needed. Johnny knew it was God and took the $10,000 check and paid the house current. Oh, I forgot to tell you that the $10,000 was money on top of the list price.

So, Johnny and Candi moved to Ohio and settled in a rented home. They got involved with Faith Life Church, and Johnny jumped into the financial business with renewed vigor. But now they had a new problem. They only had one car, and Johnny needed it to cover the many appointments he ran during the week meeting clients. Well, they knew what to do. They sowed a seed for a new car and believed they received it when they prayed according to Mark 11:24. Then the most unusual thing happened.

A childhood friend of Johnny's called and said these words. "Johnny, did I ever pay you back for that bicycle you gave me in sixth grade?" "No," Johnny said. Then his friend said, "Well, I am going to pay you back now. I am going to buy you a BMW." As kids, the two boys always talked about cars, and he knew that Johnny always wanted a BMW. The friend was true to his word and wired Johnny the money to buy himself a BMW. Once Johnny got the money, though, he realized that with a growing family now, a BMW was not the car he really needed. Eventually, he and Candi decided on getting Candi a family SUV and then a smaller car for Johnny's business driving since Candi's small car they were driving at the time was old and had problems. So that is what happened. I can remember the night that Johnny called me. He was sitting in his new car in his driveway next to Candi's new

SUV with tears in his eyes as he told me how shocked he was to have two paid for cars for the first time in his life. Johnny was a new person. He knew that God could do anything.

One day, he came by my office and said that he was tired of renting a house, that he and Candi wanted a farm with land, and they were looking. Well, I knew that Johnny's credit was not good due to the wreck and encouraged him to just rent a bit longer and build his cash reserve to allow time for his credit score to rise. But Johnny did not seem to pay much attention to what I said. He then told me that he had seen a farm down the street from me that was for sale, and he was going to check into buying it. Of course, since I owned a mortgage company at the time, I knew there was no way that Johnny would be able to qualify for that farm. I also knew he did not have the down payment for such a purchase.

However, I was shocked a week later when he walked back into my office with a grin and said the farm was his. When he told me that, I knew this was a story I had to hear. Of course, he and Candi had sown a financial seed into the work of God as they had been taught, believing they had received when they prayed. Then Johnny went on and explained to me what had happened. He went to see his bank about the purchase, and the manager pulled his credit report and sat down with him and said the following, "Johnny, you were right about your credit. You do not qualify to buy anything." But then the manager said something strange. He pushed the credit report to the side and said, "But I like you. Let me see what I can do."

To make a long story a little shorter, the bank financed 100% of the purchase, they gave him four months until his current lease ran out to move in, they filled the propane tank, paid the outstanding property taxes, and gave Johnny a $5,000 check at closing to fix the crack in the front porch's concrete. I sat there stunned as Johnny just kept going on about the Kingdom. "Wow!" was all I could say.

A month later, Johnny told me that he had sown a seed for a Ford tractor. He told me that he decided he needed a tractor on his new farm and had sown a very specific seed for a blue diesel Ford tractor. Again, since he worked for me and knowing the price of tractors, I knew that he did not yet have that kind of money. But sure enough, a few weeks later as I looked toward the road, I saw Johnny driving a blue Ford diesel tractor toward his house. When I asked him where and how he got the tractor, he said a woman randomly walked up to him at church and asked him if he knew anyone that might need a tractor. They were liquidating her parents' farm, and there was this tractor they were trying to get rid of. Johnny told her he was interested. Well, she told him not to worry about paying her, to just pay when he could, she was in no hurry. So, he had his tractor.

His success continued. The next month, he made $72,000 in just one month. If you would ask Johnny how that happened, he would say it happened by being generous toward God and understanding the laws of the Kingdom.

I can still remember sitting down with Johnny and Candi in their Georgia home with them being $5,000 behind on their bills, facing Christmas and another round of $5,000 bills coming up with no money. To help them, I simply had to help them see God through the haze of circumstances that faced them. I showed them what we have been talking about, 2 Corinthians 9:10-11.

Now he who supplies seed to the sower and bread for food will also supply and increase your store of seed and will enlarge the harvest of your righteousness. You will be enriched in every way so that you can be generous on every occasion, and through us your generosity will result in thanksgiving to God.
—2 Corinthians 9:10-11

Paul is saying that God is going to not only supply what you need to be generous, but He is also going to provide the bread you need for your own needs. Bread is referring to all that you need personally in your life. From that, He is going to increase your ability to give even more. That means you are going to increase. Again, what is the fear in giving? That you will run short for your own needs. But here God says He gives seed to the sower and the bread for food.

Now here is a very important question. Is what you have in your hand seed or is it food? You know what? It is your choice; it is your seed.

My mom's dad, my grandpa, was a farmer all his life. I remember as a young boy playing in his seed wagon. You see, every year at harvest Grandpa always kept back enough seed to fill a wagon he had in the barn. That wagon was the seed he was saving to plant in the spring for the next year's crop. During the winter months, Grandpa had to look at that big wagon brimming full of soybeans, knowing he had a choice to sell it for an immediate need or to save it for spring planting where he knew it would produce a big harvest. He had a choice, but he was convinced of the laws that governed seed time and harvest, and he staked his life on them.

Johnny and Candi had to face that same decision holding that

$160 check. They sure could have used it to pay a pressing need, but instead, they knew that being generous toward God would give them a bigger harvest in the long run. And they were correct.

> *One person gives freely, yet gains even more; another withholds unduly, but comes to poverty.*
>
> —Proverbs 11:24

There is another parable that Jesus told that I think we should look at while we are in this chapter, Matthew 25.

> *Again, it will be like a man going on a journey, who called his servants and entrusted his wealth to them. To one he gave five bags of gold, to another two bags, and to another one bag, each according to his ability. Then he went on his journey. The man who had received five bags of gold went at once and put his money to work and gained five bags more. So also, the one with two bags of gold gained two more. But the man who had received one bag went off, dug a hole in the ground and hid his master's money.*
>
> *After a long time the master of those servants returned and settled accounts with them. The man who had received five bags of gold brought the other five. "Master," he said, "you entrusted me with five bags of gold. See, I have gained five more."*
>
> *His master replied, "Well done, good and faithful servant! You have been faithful with a few things; I will put you in charge of many things. Come and share your master's happiness!"*
>
> *"The man with two bags of gold also came. "Master," he said, "you entrusted me with two bags of gold; see, I have gained two more."*

His master replied, "Well done, good and faithful servant! You have been faithful with a few things; I will put you in charge of many things. Come and share your master's happiness!"

"Then the man who had received one bag of gold came. "Master," he said, "I knew that you are a hard man, harvesting where you have not sown and gathering where you have not scattered seed. So I was afraid and went out and hid your gold in the ground. See, here is what belongs to you."

His master replied, "You wicked, lazy servant! So you knew that I harvest where I have not sown and gather where I have not scattered seed? Well then, you should have put my money on deposit with the bankers, so that when I returned I would have received it back with interest. So take the bag of gold from him and give it to the one who has ten bags. For whoever has will be given more, and they will have an abundance. Whoever does not have, even what they have will be taken from them. And throw that worthless servant outside, into the darkness, where there will be weeping and gnashing of teeth."

—Matthew 25:14-30

The story is a familiar one. The master is leaving town and leaves three servants in charge. To one, he gives five bags of gold; to one, he gives two bags of gold; and to one, he gives one bag of gold. The first two get to work immediately and double the bags of gold they have. The master applauds them for their work. But it is the third servant that I want to look at. Let's take a close look at what this servant tells the master when he is giving an account of what he has done with the master's gold.

> *Then the man who had received one bag of gold came. "Master," he said, "I knew that you are a hard man, harvesting where you have not sown and gathering where you have not scattered seed. So I was afraid and went out and hid your gold in the ground. See, here is what belongs to you."*

Pay close attention to the first sentence, "*Master, I knew that you were a hard man, harvesting where you have not sown and gathering where you have not scattered seed.*" What is he saying? I will tell you exactly what he is saying. "Who is paying for the seed? If you are harvesting where you have not planted seed, well, someone had to plant that seed." Now, that is not what the master was asking him to do as he gave him the money to buy seed. But that was how the servant viewed the master, as a very hard taskmaster. Basically, his attitude was, "There is nothing in it for me, so I am not interested."

Because of his image of the master, he basically refuses to get involved. He tries to hide his true contempt for the master by stating his motive to hide the money was because he was afraid of losing it and so went and hid the money to protect it. But the master calls his bluff and says that if he really cared for the master, he would have at least put the money on deposit at the bank, and there it would have gained interest. No, the servant was not really afraid of losing the gold. He was afraid of what it would cost him to get involved.

He had a perverse and wicked image of the master. Perverse because the opposite was actually true. The master was not a hard taskmaster. The other two servants were rewarded with promotion and invited to enjoy the master's estate after they successfully worked with the master's money. This servant, because of his wrong image of the master, chose not to participate.

And this is exactly what religion teaches us—that God is a hard taskmaster and there is no profit in working with Him, so why get involved? But that image of God is totally perverse and not true. To call God unfair is wicked. God is exactly the opposite of that portrayal. He is good and a rewarder.

But now, I want to point out a very important point that is made in this story. Pay close attention to what the master does with the gold that he takes back from the wicked servant.

> *So take the bag of gold from him and give it to the one who has ten bags. For whoever has will be given more, and they will have an abundance. Whoever does not have, even what they have will be taken from them. And throw that worthless servant outside, into the darkness, where there will be weeping and gnashing of teeth.*

Did I read that right? The master took the bag of gold from the worthless servant and gave it to the one that had 10 bags and not the one that had 4? I am not sure that is politically correct, but that is God's wisdom. Listen VERY CAREFULLY!!!!

GOD IS GOING TO GIVE HIS GREAT IDEAS AND ASSIGNMENTS TO THOSE OF HIS CHILDREN WHO HAVE HIS PROFIT IN MIND AND HAVE PROVEN THEMSELVES ON THE SMALL JOBS FIRST.

God is going to give His great ideas and assignments to those of His children who have His profit in mind and have proven themselves on the small jobs first. God is not stupid. He is going to put His money where it will have the greatest return.

Please think about what I have just said: "God is going to put His money where it will have the greatest return!"

Now, God is not in the money business, but He is in the people business. As we are faithful to work diligently with Him, He will promote us and favor us with His good things. Yes, God has favorites in the sense of who He trusts with different assignments. Those who have proven themselves faithful will earn God's trust to handle bigger and more rewarding assignments for Him.

Notice the attitude of the two servants that were successful. They went at once and put their master's money to work! Why immediately? Because they knew this was an opportunity, not a weight of slavery. So many of God's people view serving God as a drudgery, a duty to be fulfilled and not the opportunity that it really is.

When Drenda and I were building the Now Center, we had to make a decision. We were a church of only about 500 when we decided that we needed to build a permanent and bigger home for our growing body of believers. We set out to raise as much money as we could toward the 6-million dollar project. This was a huge amount of money to us at the time. The plan was to build the basic infrastructure for about 4.2 million and then add the remaining 2 million dollars' worth of equipment and build-outs as the money came in.

This was not our first experience with being generous toward God's projects, but it was the biggest one we had been a part of at that time. However, like the servants in the story who knew their master's goodness, we immediately wanted to be a part of raising the money, and we wanted to give at a level that would take faith and obedience to what we believed God was telling us. On the day that the entire congregation declared what they had agreed on sowing into the project, Drenda and I said we were giving $200,000. Now at the time, we did not have the $200,000. But we had a seed of about $20,000 that we were going to sow for the remaining balance. We knew as in the past, God would show us where and how to harvest that amount with plenty left over for ourselves. After sowing what we had, we began to pray in the Spirit, waiting for direction and instruction as to where and how to capture the remaining amount of money.

To set the stage for how God brought this money in, I need to tell you that we have owned a financial company for over 30 years. That company works with various vendors and professionals, as I mentioned to you earlier. Most of the bigger vendors we work with have annual conventions and get-togethers for their clients.

This particular year, they had invited Drenda and me to come to London, England for their convention. We were staying at a very nice hotel in downtown London, and it was just lovely, as they say in London. Well, the company had one event that was on the other side of town, and the vice president of the company invited Drenda and me to ride with her in a cab to the event, which we gladly accepted. The vice president, of course, thanked us for all the business we had sent them and then began telling us about a new bonus program they were launching that year. She went on to explain how it worked and the bonus structure that they were going to pay out to the associates who recommended their product.

I was very excited as she spoke as I knew we did enough business to qualify for the bonuses she was talking about. Then abruptly, as I asked for further details, she stated that our company would not qualify for the bonus program based on the structure of our relationship with her company. I could not believe it. Why did she go through all the detail and sell me on this great plan to simply take it away from me at the last minute? And secondly, I did not understand how my relationship with her company was structured so as not to be able to qualify for the bonus. Even though I asked further questions, she did not really give me a clear answer. The only thing I knew for sure was that I would not be able to qualify for the bonus; she made that clear.

A year went by and our production was good for that year, so I had the thought to call her up and inquire again about the bonus. However, this time when I called, I could not reach her, so I left a message with her assistant with my question. The next day, her assistant called me back and, with a stern sounding voice, stated that the vice president had already told me a year earlier that I did not qualify, and there was nothing she could do about it. *Well, okay*, I thought, *at least I tried.*

Now, as I was praying about where to find this $180,000, I heard the Holy Spirit tell me to call the vice president and ask for that bonus again. I will tell you that I was not thrilled to hear that. After my experience asking her the previous two years, I knew where she stood. She made that very clear. So, I thought I would send her an email to just test the waters, so to speak. About seven days later, I received her reply which, to my joy, said she had thought about it and had decided to give my company the bonus. Amazingly, the bonus was $200,000! Now, here is the best part. That contract change has stayed in place now for the last 14 years, and I have received that $200,000 every year since. You see, God is a rewarder! And there is profit in being generous toward God's assignments.

About five years went by, and we decided that as a church we needed to raise more money to complete a few things at the church and to buy some equipment. Again, we had to decide how much we wanted to sow toward those projects, and we decided on $500,000. Wow, that was a lot of money, but we felt we could trust God with it after seeing what He did with the $200,000. Again, we sowed what we could, which I think was $50,000, and were believing for the Holy Spirit to show us where and how to capture the remaining $450,000. I think maybe six weeks went by, and I received a notice that there were going to be a few contractual changes on how we were to be paid in our company. After we calculated the changes that were taking place, we would make about $630,000 more over the next three years than we had been making. Pretty cool, right? Well, guess what? That contractual change has stayed in place now for the last 11 years, and we get that increase every year. God is a God of profit. He is good and is a rewarder.

YOU TAKE CARE OF GOD'S BUSINESS, AND HE WILL TAKE CARE OF YOURS!

Again, let me say it one more time. You take care of God's business, and He will take care of yours!

Chapter 13

THE LAW OF CELEBRATION

It seems most people these days do not have much to celebrate as it seems to be the same old thing day after day. And that is too bad, because life should be a party celebrating the goodness of God every single day. But I understand. When you are struggling just to survive, it is hard to celebrate. But celebrating is part of your answer, the key to your get out of jail card. Let me begin our conversation by asking you a question.

What are you celebrating?

Celebration should be a part of everything you do and plan to do.

Let's go back to the discussion we had previously where I was telling you about the trips and bonuses the vendors in my financial company offered. The trips they offered were pretty amazing with all-expense paid luxury accommodations in some of the most exotic and beautiful places in the world. You know that those trips cost the companies hundreds of thousands of dollars to provide, so why do they do it? Well, of course they have their products they want to get out to the public, but they could just make the products available through an online website or through TV ads. But in their experience, they found that people need help understanding how their products work and it is in the company's best interest to provide that information.

In their research, they found that a conversation with a real person proved to be the most effective way to communicate this information to the consumer. So, these companies hire salespeople to do just that. But there are hundreds of financial products out there, so how are the financial companies going to inspire sales agents to offer their particular product? There are many ways to do that.

Having the most competitive product or a product that does a better job of meeting the consumer's needs than a competitor is certainly one way of doing that. Commissions paid out to the sales agents being higher than a competitors is also a good way to inspire people to sell their product. But competition is fierce among companies, and there are a lot of great companies with great products, all which would be good for the client. So how do you inspire the sales agents to pick your company's product to use with their clients? This is where the incentive trip comes into play.

The sales reps that are selling these financial products are not typically tied to a captive agent sales contract, meaning that these salespeople are free to pick any company and product they want when providing products to their clients.

So, let's assume that there are several great products that pretty much have the same quality and benefit to your client at roughly the same price. Let's assume that most of these companies have no trip incentive program but one does. And let's say that the one company that has an incentive program is providing a trip to Bora Bora for their sales reps who do a certain amount of production with them for that year. Assuming everything else is equal, same value and the same price to the client, which company are you going to pick for your client? I think the answer to that is a no-brainer. So even though the other companies have great products, at the same cost as the one you are choosing, they did not get the business. Why not?

Let's analyze how the one company with the incentive program got the business. This company that was selling the product with the incentive program understands human nature. They set a goal and also set a reward. Please write this down.

Set the goal, and set a reward.

Now let's just change the word reward to the word celebration. Why? Because the word celebration carries a more thrilling and detailed image of what I am trying to get across.

Set the goal, and set a celebration.

It is a fact that most sales reps will push themselves past their normal pace to reach a goal that qualifies them for a reward. I have been in sales all of my life and have always loved reaching for the production level that would allow me to attend one of these amazing trips or receive bonuses. As I would be working through the year, I would always imagine myself at the location of that year's trip. I would imagine just how great it would be to be there. That goal would push me past my normal comfortable pace into a new level of activity. When I finally arrived at the company convention and was honored to receive that trip and the bonus check, it was a great feeling. It was not only that I had qualified for the trip, but also I had great satisfaction in what I had been able to accomplish in that business year.

The company providing the incentive trip was smart. They did not wait until after I had actually qualified for the trip to tell me about the trip. "Hey, you did a great job this year. We are going to reward you with a trip to Bora Bora." No, that is not how they would do it. They would tell you three or four months before the qualification year began, along with the details on how to qualify.

Why? So you could adjust your strategy and processes, if necessary, to enable you to reach that goal.

I told you my story of how God led me into sales after college and how hard it was for me. I was so shy. Having to make those phone calls and talk to people for a living was so out of my comfort zone. Although I hated making the calls, I did love the financial business as a business. I loved learning all about financial products, the economy, and being part of a crusade to help people. But it was tough; I wanted to quit every day. I know you are thinking, *Well, if you hated it, then how did you get involved with it?*

During college and just after college, I was working at a retail store that sold window coverings, like curtains and mini blinds, and various types of floor coverings. I was the window installer in the operation. One day as I was preparing an order for installation, the owner's insurance agent came in to talk to him about some insurance matters. I could not help but overhear the conversation, and strangely, I was fascinated.

Shortly after that, a man who I had never met called me and said he was looking to hire representatives for a new company in the area that worked in the financial field. My name had been given to him by someone who knew that I was looking for something new. He told me that he was conducting a meeting at such and such address on such and such date, and if I was interested in finding out more, I should come. Well, I was interested, so I went to the meeting. What I learned at that meeting was fascinating, and something went off on the inside of me that said, *Yes, I want to do this*. But remember, I was called by God to preach His Word. What about that?

Well, at the time this happened, I had just asked Drenda to marry me; and we had set a trip to drive down to Georgia, where she was from. I had already met her family—as they came out to Tulsa once—but this would be the first time I would be going to Georgia, and I wanted to ask her father for her hand in marriage.

While there, I was going to visit her home church with her. I will admit I was a little confused as to what to do about this offer to work in this financial business. There was something in me that so wanted to do it even though it seemed so out of character for me. After the Sunday morning service, a woman who I did not know, but Drenda certainly did, walked up to me and said she had a word for me. She said, "You are looking at a job offer. The Lord showed me 10 points in regard to this position," and she named everything I would be doing at this new job. She said, "You are to take this job, and the Lord is in it."

So with that, I took the position and started training. It was so crazy. I had this strong desire to learn this field and work with clients, yet at the same time, I was so timid and afraid to talk to people. It was a real battle for me to step into it. But that prophetic word that I received at that church verified to me that God was in this, and I knew it was the direction I was to go, even though it did not make sense to me in my mind.

So Drenda and I were married, and we were living strictly on commissions. Wow, that was a struggle. In that first year, the company I was selling for had an incentive trip to the Boca Raton Resort in Boca Raton, Florida. The fact that they were having this convention did not even catch my attention. I had never traveled and had never been to a resort before. And being brand-new in the business, I thought there was no way I was even going to come close. My say no before you say yes training just dismissed this as an impossible possibility. Besides, I was having enough trouble and stress just struggling to make enough money to pay the bills.

But Drenda had a completely different view of life. She was the class president of her class of 500 all four years of high school. She had a four-point grade average and was the valedictorian of her graduating class. She was also the annual editor for her school paper. We were polar opposites when it came to drive and ambition at that time.

When Drenda saw that video advertising this trip, she got so excited and said, "We are going!" I disagreed, saying there was no way we could make that trip, the production level was just too high. But she would not relent. She would make me watch the company promo video every single day, and she posted a brochure on my desk about the trip as well. At first, the video did not interest me. But it was her passion that finally got me thinking about it. So I calculated how much business we would have to do for the remainder of the contest period to make it, and I still thought it was impossible, but I would not rule it out.

As we came down to the last two months, we were running short but, surprisingly, not as short as I thought we would be at that point. As we were discussing the situation, Drenda then told me that she would get her license to help. By the time she went through the testing period for the license, it was then the last month of the contest period. She went out and met a couple of families that we knew and wrote a couple of cases, which along with what I was doing helped us get closer.

It came down to the last night of the contest, and we were two cases short. I was meeting a client that night, and so was she. We were to meet at the Federal Express office to overnight our paperwork out as it had to be at the home office by the next day to count for the contest. The Federal Express office closes at 11:00 p.m., and I got there just a few minutes before closing time hoping that Drenda would already be there, but she wasn't. Now, this was before cell phones came out, so there was no way for me to call to find out where she was. I knew her appointment was at 7:00 p.m., and she should have been finished with it long before then.

As the clock ticked toward the 11:00 p.m. closing time, I became concerned, not only about the case but about her. The agent at the desk said they had to close exactly at 11:00 p.m. to get all their packages out to the airport on time. At two minutes till 11:00 p.m., Drenda came flying in the parking lot and made it inside the door before closing. We hurriedly filled out all the forms and gave them to the desk agent and were so excited that we went and each had a coke at a local late-night restaurant. Why only two cokes? Because that was all the money we had with us. But WE DID IT! We qualified to go all-expenses paid to that amazing resort. That was the first time I had ever been to a resort or sat at dinner with white tablecloths and many more firsts.

My life was literally changed, and my vision for our lives was never the same because of that trip. That is why I said I am changing the word reward to celebration in my above statement. It was truly a celebration unlike anything I had ever experienced before. But how did we get there? Of course, God was working with us, but it was the incentive, the promised celebration, that motivated us to push past anything either of us had ever done before.

SO REMEMBER, SET THE GOAL, AND SET THE CELEBRATION.

Oh, I only wish that you would experience the joy of celebration that I did that week. And you know what? I believe you can! So remember, set the goal, and set the celebration.

Yet, this is not how most companies operate. They give bonuses that are tied to years of service. What kind of incentive does that provide? You want to celebrate that this employee hung on for a certain amount of time? Is this why you hired them, to put in the time? Or did you hire them to get things done? Remember, you want to celebrate a clear goal that will validate why you hired this person in the first place. Does just putting in the time pay the bills? I am sure you already found out that it does just the opposite.

Some companies give raises based on how the employee performs throughout the year, which sounds great. Their mistake is in not laying out a reward that is based on measurable qualifiers and not having a clearly defined celebration if they accomplish it in a set time frame as directed. Of course, this should be covered with the employee before the actual time period begins, not at the end or in the middle.

Then I see other companies give out automatic raises based on current cost of living data from the U.S government. That is fine for maintaining or keeping your employees but not for motivational purposes. You will never motivate an employee by offering a way to just pay their bills. Set goals for your teams, and then follow through with a great celebration.

In the early days of our church, I think we were running 500 people, and we told our staff that once we started hitting 1,600 a weekend, we would take all of them to Hawaii. We kept that goal before them, and that is exactly what we did. When we reached 1,600, we took all of our full-time staff to Hawaii for a week. It was an awesome trip.

But looking back, I should have made smaller, more achievable goals along the way with a smaller celebration. The gap from 500 to 1,600 was too great a gap to cover in the period of time that I had hoped for, and many gave up on achieving it. There is an art to setting goals—enough to motivate but not so far out that your team thinks it is impossible. Remember, small goals add up to big wins.

When I first started out in sales, our office would have a big board with every sales rep on it and the production they had submitted each week. Our sales meetings were always motivational, and we would hand out T-shirts to recognize the leaders each month. You would not believe how those reps fought for those T-shirts! I learned that recognition meant more to most of them than the money did.

...SMALL GOALS ADD UP TO BIG WINS.

I found that people want to compete; they want to win. They just want a clear path to do so. THERE HAS TO BE A REWARD! People must know if they fight it out, there is a reward, a celebration just around the corner.

Although I understand why most companies pay through a salary system, I strongly suggest that you reevaluate how your pay plan works. God made us to create, and He gave us an imagination. We function best knowing that we have an unlimited future. By getting your people involved in working toward goals, you tap into their imagination and creativity. You will find that the answers you have been looking for all along are there in your people, but you must prime the pump to get it out. What incentive does a salaried person have to go beyond the paycheck? Should it be a fear-based incentive program? That if you do not produce, you may not be here tomorrow? Or should it be, "Hey, you do this, and we are going to reward you with this"?

Salaries do not motivate by themselves. Think about it; your employee knows he will get paid his normal paycheck whether he gets involved or not. Eventually, they ask themselves why they should keep pushing so hard; it does not change their paycheck. If they slow down or speed up, no difference. This system will not work! So, the employer thinks, *Okay, I will raise this person's pay. This will motivate them to work harder and take on more responsibility.* Wrong. You are still not operating on a system of incentive. Once people are in a position, they set their pace at a management level, managing their position with a processing mentality. A processing mentality processes what they are told to do, what they must do.

YOU DO NOT WANT YOUR PEOPLE TO OPERATE WITH A PROCESSING MENTALITY!

You want people to operate with an entrepreneur's mentality. No entrepreneur dreams of starting their business just so they can have a job. No, they start their business so they will have an unlimited future. They put the time in to start the business because they are motivated by the reward of freedom and prosperity. Secondly, the person that starts their own business is not looking for an easier life. I know, because as an entrepreneur, I work more hours than anyone would ever pay me for. Why? Because I have a vision and a passion for what I do. My future is not punching a clock just to put my time in; this is what I want to do. This is who I am, and I love it.

The employers I know are all talking about how hard it is to find people who own their position just as the owner would. They tell me that everyone seems to have a hireling attitude. I agree, and the reason your people all act like hirelings is because you pay people like they are hirelings. Now, again, I am not talking about the amount you pay them. I said the way you pay them. They typically are paid a salary with no ownership or profit from what they are building. How discouraging is that?

Here is the sad part: Because they do not get to share in the profit of what they are building with you, they are all behind-the-scenes, behind your back, planning their escape to freedom. The creativity they so long to let loose is being used after hours thinking of ways to build their business, not yours. Eventually, they will leave. The sad thing is they left mentally long before they actually left your employment. So, if you want to build something that will last, you must allow your people to share in the joy, the celebration of building something. Something that benefits and rewards them for their labor and vision. If you don't, you are simply training your competition. So, let's remember what we said in the beginning.

Set the goal, and set the celebration, the reward.

One last thing: You can't inflate a balloon with holes in it, no matter how hard you try. Let me show you one of my favorite Scriptures, and then I will explain what I mean.

> *Praise the Lord, my soul; all my inmost being, praise his holy name. Praise the Lord, my soul, and forget not all his benefits—who forgives all your sins and heals all your diseases, who redeems your life from the pit and crowns you with love and compassion, who satisfies your desires with good things so that your youth is renewed like the eagles.*
>
> —Psalm 103:1-5

Notice it says when a desire is satisfied, it renews your strength! You are not the only one on your team who has desires. Setting up a system of compensation that rewards your employees for what they do—instead of the box their name is written on, on the corporation spreadsheet—will totally invigorate your team and your future. It is not wrong to pay a person a salary as long as you offer a system that pays out bonuses, or profit sharing, or some system of pay which rewards people based on what they just did, not on what they were supposed to do. It must have a detailed goal and reward structure that is communicated to those involved. Having times of celebration renews your strength and theirs! It makes you and your team want to do it again. They determine that the reward is worth the price. Labor with no reward, however, does just the opposite, as seen in every nation that has tried socialism.

Look at Venezuela, a nation that was the richest nation in South America at one time. Amazingly, Venezuela has the largest known oil reserves in the world, more than Saudi Arabia, yet it is basically a bankrupt nation. Let me quote a portion of an article that I recently read that clearly shows what happens when you remove all reward for hard labor from a country.

> *When Hugo Chavez was elected President, one of his first actions was to start nationalizing the agriculture sector, supposedly reducing poverty and inequality by taking from rich landowners to give to poor workers. From 1999 to 2016, his regime robbed more than 6 million hectares of land from its rightful owners.*
>
> *Nationalization destroyed production in affected industries because no government has the capacity to run thousands of businesses or the profit motive to run them efficiently. Instead, government officials face incentives to please voters by selling products at low prices and hiring more employees than necessary, even when that's the wrong industry decision.*
>
> *As economic theory predicted, as state control of the agricultural industry increased, Venezuela's food production*

> *fell 75% in two decades while the country's population increased by 33%. This was a recipe for shortages and economic disaster. After agriculture, the regime nationalized electricity, water, oil, banks, supermarkets, construction, and other crucial sectors. And in all these sectors, the government increased payrolls and gave away products at low cost, resulting in days-long countrywide blackouts, frequent water service interruptions, falling oil production, and bankrupt government enterprises.*[28]

Labor with no reward does not promote productivity, just the opposite. God knows this. This is how He made us—to not only work but also to enjoy the fruit of our labor. Even Jesus understood the principle of setting the goal and then setting the celebration.

> *Give, and it will be given to you. A good measure, pressed down, shaken together and running over, will be poured into your lap. For with the measure you use, it will be measured to you.*
>
> —Luke 6:38

Notice how much time is devoted to explaining the result of giving. God could have simply said, "I am God. GIVE!" No, that would not work. Then men would resent God, and He would be no different than the socialistic governments we see in the world. God would become a hard taskmaster.

Paul understood this same principle.

---

28. Daniel Di Martino, "How Socialism Destroyed Venezuela," https://economics21.org, March 21, 2019

This is what I mean: The one who sows sparingly will also reap sparingly. The one who sows generously will also reap generously. Each one should give as he has determined in his heart, not reluctantly or under pressure, for God loves a cheerful giver.

God is able to make all grace overflow to you, so that in all things, at all times, having all that you need, you will overflow in every good work. As it is written: "He scattered; he gave to the poor. His righteousness remains forever."

And he who provides seed to the sower and bread for food will provide and multiply your seed for sowing, and will increase the harvest of your righteousness. You will be made rich in every way so that you may be generous in every way, which produces thanksgiving to God through us.

—2 Corinthians 9:6-11 (EHV)

Again, we see that the goal was laid out clearly along with the reward or celebration also being laid out clearly. Again, we see more time and detail explaining the reward and celebration than the instruction to give. If that is the system that God uses with us, I think we might do better if we use the same system for all those that report to us in whatever endeavor we may be involved with.

Again, first set the goal, and secondly, set the celebration, what the reward will be if the goal is fulfilled as directed and on time. You leave the creativity up to them on how to accomplish the mission. Do not allow yourself to micromanage their process. They will surprise you and themselves.

I said I would tell you what I meant by trying to blow up a balloon with holes in. It is impossible. I said it was impossible, right? Unfortunately, this is how many leaders operate. Instead of fixing the holes, they think if they just try harder, and invest more money, everything will turn out great. But, of course, they find out that is not true. So stop and fix the system. Putting new people or more money into the balloon will not fix it. The people and the money will just be lost through the same dysfunctions that caused the last ones to leave. You can fix it; God will help you.

The law of celebration—everyone loves a party!

CONCLUSION

I hope you have enjoyed this book, but more importantly, I hope there were a few things that spoke to you, encouraged you, and will help you accelerate in your own life and occupation. As I said in the beginning of this book, there are many other laws for acceleration that could have been written. But these are the ones that I saw in my dream, the ones that the Holy Spirit told me that I would need to learn and implement if I was going reach the goals the Lord has set for my life.

In conclusion, there are two laws that I want to mention that are higher than any law I may have mentioned in this book. They are:

> *Jesus replied: "'Love the Lord your God with all your heart and with all your soul and with all your mind.' This is the first and greatest commandment. And the second is like it: 'Love your neighbor as yourself.' All the Law and the Prophets hang on these two commandments."*
>
> —Matthew 22:37-40

FAITH APPENDIX

What is faith?

Faith is a term that Christians throw around loosely. And I am convinced that many, if not the majority, do not know what faith is, why it is needed, how to know if they are in faith, and how to find faith. If faith is the switch that healed the woman in Matthew 9:20-22, as Jesus stated, then we need to take a very close look at faith! We find our definition of faith in Romans 4:18-21. Oh, I know what you are thinking, *No, Gary. Hebrews 11:1 is our definition of faith.*

> *Faith is being sure about what we hope for, convinced about things we do not see.*
>
> —Hebrews 11:1 (EHV)

Yes, that is the traditional answer, but if you look at the Scripture, Hebrews 11:1 is telling us the benefits of faith, not what faith actually is. I believe our Scripture in Romans will give us a very clear picture of what faith actually is.

> *Against all hope, Abraham in hope believed and so became the father of many nations, just as it had been said to him, "So shall your offspring be." Without weakening in his faith,*

> *he faced the fact that his body was as good as dead—since he was about a hundred years old—and that Sarah's womb was also dead. Yet he did not waver through unbelief regarding the promise of God, but was strengthened in his faith and gave glory to God, being fully persuaded that God had power to do what he had promised.*
>
> —Romans 4:18-21

Let's understand the setting of this story. Abraham and Sarah could not have children. I do not mean they were having trouble conceiving a child and should keep trying. I mean they were almost 100 years of age, and it was over. Their bodies could not have children; it was impossible! Yet God promised Abraham a child even though in the natural it was utterly impossible. The Bible says that Abraham was fully persuaded that God had the power to do what He said, in spite of the natural facts that stated a different story.

> ***"FAITH IS BEING SURE ABOUT WHAT WE HOPE FOR, CONVINCED ABOUT THINGS WE DO NOT SEE."***
> **—HEBREWS 11:1 (EHV)**

Here then is our definition of faith: "being fully persuaded that God has the power to do what He has promised." I state it this way: **Being in agreement with heaven**, not just mentally but fully persuaded, our hearts settled and convinced totally of what God has said, in spite of the natural realm indicating something else.

Our definition of what faith is:

Faith is being fully persuaded of what God says! It is our hearts and minds being in agreement with heaven, our hearts being fully persuaded, confident, and at rest.

Why is faith needed?

Why can't God just heal everyone in the hospital when He wants to? Why can't He stop wars? Why can't He send angels to preach the Gospel to us? I am sure you have heard all of these questions before. The answer is that He can't. It is not that God does not have the ability to do so. He does not have the jurisdiction or the authority to do so. "Gary, are you saying that God cannot do whatever He wants to?" I know this sounds really strange to you right now, but let's look at the Bible to find our answer to that one.

> *But there is a place where someone has testified:*
>
> *"What is man that you are mindful of them, a son of man that you care for them? You made them a little lower than the angels; you crowned them with glory and honor and put everything under their feet."*
>
> *In putting everything under them, God left nothing that is not subject to them. Yet at present we do not see everything subject to them.*
>
> —Hebrews 2:6-8

We can see from this Scripture that God gave man complete legal jurisdiction over the entire earth realm when he was placed here. There was nothing that was not under his jurisdiction. He ruled over this realm with absolute jurisdiction and authority. His ability to rule with authority was backed up by the government which had set him here. In essence, he ruled with the delegated authority of the Kingdom of God. He wore the crown of that government, which represented the glory of God, the anointing, and the position of honor that he bore.

To get a good picture of what this looks like, think of a natural king. Although he is a natural man and bears no real power in his natural being, he wears a crown that signifies he stands in representation of not only himself but also an entire kingdom and government. His words carry authority only because they are backed up by all the power and natural resources of the government and kingdom he represents.

If you think of a sheriff directing traffic, he will stop a massive tractor-trailer truck with a command, "Stop in the name of the law." Yes, the truck is much bigger than the man, and the man, in himself, is no match for the truck, but the truck stops. It stops not because of the man but because of the badge the man wears, which represents a government. In this case, the government is much bigger than the man who wears the badge. For the truck driver, there is no fear of the man, but there is a fear of the government that the man represents, causing the truck to stop.

The same is true here. Adam ruled over everything that was created in the earth realm. God's power and dominion, represented by the crown of glory and honor, gave man the assurance that his words ruled on behalf of the Kingdom of God.

It is very important to note that when Adam lost his ability to rule over the earth by committing treason against God's government, he lost his crown. The earth realm became tainted and changed. Death entered the earth realm, and Satan then had a legal claim of authority and influence in the affairs of men. It is imperative that you also understand that man is still the legal ruler over the earth realm, as God has placed him in that position, but he now has no authority to rule spiritually as he once had. Even in his fallen state, however, he is still in charge of the earth. Yes, he no longer has his crown of God's government to back him up. He has no authority to rule with God's power and glory; he has lost his position of honor. But he is still the only legal door to the earth realm. This is why God has to use Spirit-filled people to bring about His will in the lives of men.

THIS IS WHY GOD HAS TO USE SPIRIT-FILLED PEOPLE TO BRING ABOUT HIS WILL IN THE LIVES OF MEN.

In the same way, Satan uses demon-inspired people to affect the earth realm toward his plan for man. This principle of man's jurisdiction over the earth is vital to your understanding of Kingdom law, and once you understand it, it will answer many questions you may have in the future as to why certain things happen, or why certain things did not or do not happen spiritually.

You may say, "But I thought God owned the earth and the fullness thereof?" True, He does. I hope this example will help you understand what I am saying. If I leased a home that I owned to you, although I legally owned the home, I legally gave up the right to drop by anytime I wanted to. There is a clause in most leases that specifies when landlords may legally enter rented premises—for example, to deal with an emergency or to make repairs—and the amount of notice required. If I tried to enter the home outside of this agreement, it would be considered breaking and entering, even if I owned the property. If I violated the law specified in the lease, I could then be legally forced to vacate the premises even though I owned it. This illustrates why Satan had to go through Adam to gain access to the earth realm. Only Adam had the key! Satan had to go through the door, and Adam was it. If Satan tried to go around Adam, he would have legally been forced out.

> *The devil led him up to a high place and showed him in an instant all the kingdoms of the world. And he said to him, "I will give you all their authority and splendor, for it has been given to me, and I can give it to anyone I want to. So if you worship me, it will all be yours."*
>
> —Luke 4:5-7

You can see in this verse that Satan claims that the authority and splendor (wealth) of the kingdoms of men have been given to him. Who gave him this authority? The one who had it, Adam! Thus God cannot just burst into the affairs of men without going through a legal entrance. If He did, Satan would claim foul play. No, God would have to go through the same door that Satan used to bring His government and authority to bear in the earth, and that was a man. But was there such a man?

> *The Lord had said to Abram, "Go from your country, your people and your father's household and go to the land I will show you. I will make you into a great nation, and I will bless you; I will make your name great, and you will be a blessing. I will bless those who bless you, and whoever curses you I will curse; and all peoples on earth will be blessed through you."*
>
> —Genesis 12:1-3

Abraham is called the father of our faith because he is the man that opened the door of the earth realm to God whereby all nations on the earth would be blessed. Of course, when this verse speaks of the nations being blessed, it is speaking of Jesus Christ, who would later make a way for the government of God to once again have legal access to the earth realm through the faith of Abraham.

Abraham's faith opened a legal doorway for heaven, which God locked permanently open by making a legal agreement (covenant) with Abraham and his seed or heirs.

"CONSEQUENTLY, FAITH COMES FROM HEARING THE MESSAGE, AND THE MESSAGE IS HEARD THROUGH THE WORD ABOUT CHRIST."
—ROMANS 10:17

Let me paraphrase what I am saying. The government of heaven can only gain its access into the earth realm through a man or a woman on the earth because they have legal jurisdiction there. That legality can only be accomplished if a man or woman is totally persuaded in their heart of what God says (faith).

Another way to say it is that heaven can only legally affect a man or woman in the earth realm who desires and chooses to come under God's dominion and authority. This would be the same principle that Satan used to gain access into the earth, using Adam to do so. He convinced Adam that God could not be trusted and brought Adam's heart out of agreement with God. Consequently, Adam chose to believe Satan and rejected God's authority.

This is the same principle that God would then use to bring His government and authority back into the earth realm through Abraham. Abraham believed God, and his agreement was counted by God as righteousness, meaning that the required legal agreement was there. This agreement by both parties, God and Abraham, allowed God to put a legal contract (a covenant) in place that secured heaven's access into the earth realm, BUT it is vital to note that this agreement only affected Abraham and his heirs. A sign of this covenant was given to all of Abraham's heirs, which was circumcision. Circumcision was the cutting off of the foreskin from the male penis. As a man planted his seed in a woman, his seed had to pass through that circumcised penis, which declared to Satan and the father and mother themselves that this child stood before heaven as an heir of that legal agreement that God and Abraham had put in place.

As we read previously, however, each man or woman, although having that legal agreement available to them, still had to fulfill the legal requirement of their own heart being fully persuaded of what God said to actually enjoy the personal benefits of that agreement that God and Abraham made. In essence, the covenant ran the wires to their house, but they still had to turn on the switch by believing and acting on the Word of God personally.

Okay, we now know what faith is and why faith is legally required. It is now imperative that we know how to get faith and how to know if we are in faith.

How do we get faith?

Here is a clue: You can't pray for faith. Surprised? I thought so.

> *Consequently, faith comes from hearing the message, and the message is heard through the word about Christ.*
>
> —Romans 10:17

How does faith come by hearing the Word of God? Is that all there is to it? What is the process? Is just hearing the Word all it takes for faith to be developed in the human spirit? To understand how faith comes and what Romans 10:17 is talking about, we can look to Mark chapter 4. If you throw your Bible up in the air, it should land open to Mark chapter 4; it is that important! Jesus said in Mark 4:13 that if you did not understand what He was teaching in this chapter, you would not be able to understand any other parable in the Bible. I would say that is pretty important!

Why is this chapter so important? It is because it tells us how heaven interfaces into the earth realm, how it gains legality, and where that takes place. Nothing is more important to your life than knowing what this whole chapter is talking about. "How does the Kingdom of God operate?" you may ask. Read Mark chapter 4! In this chapter, Jesus tells us three parables regarding how faith is produced in the human spirit, which as you know now, is a requirement for heaven to legally invade Earth.

The three stories in this chapter are the parable of the sower, the parable of the man scattering seed, and the story of the mustard seed.

Let's begin by first looking at the second story Jesus tells in Mark chapter 4, the story of the man scattering seed.

> *He also said, "This is what the Kingdom of God is like. A man scatters seed on the ground. Night and day, whether he sleeps or gets up, the seed sprouts and grows, though he does not know how. All by itself the soil produces grain—first the stalk, then the head, then the full kernel in the head. As soon as the grain is ripe, he puts the sickle to it, because the harvest has come."*
>
> —Mark 4:26-29

Before we jump into this passage, let's first define our terms. What is the seed Jesus is talking about, and what is the ground? Jesus actually defines those terms in the preceding parable of the sower in the same chapter. The seed is the Word of God, and the ground is the heart of man or the spirit of man. So in this parable, using Jesus's own definition of those two words, we would say that Jesus is saying a man scatters the Word of God into his own heart. Then all by itself the soil or the heart of man starts to produce faith (agreement with heaven) in the earth realm.

Before I go forward, it is critical that you remember what our definition of faith is: the heart of a man or woman firmly persuaded of what heaven says. This passage says that although the man does not know how the process works, the Word that was sown into his heart begins to grow and produce agreement all by itself. This happens if he sleeps or is awake; it does not matter, the process continues. As the man keeps the Word in his heart, slowly his heart is coming into agreement with what heaven says, and faith is being produced.

Our Scripture reference in Mark chapter 4 tells us that the heart produces agreement through a process. The story tells us that at first when our heart receives the Word, faith begins to form. Jesus compares that phase to a sprout. The sprout then goes on and continues to grow and becomes a stalk. Eventually, the head forms on the stalk, but even at this late phase, there is no fruit, no agreement, and no change in the natural realm. Then Jesus says the process continues as the head then matures and produces mature grain. When the process reaches that point, when the mature seed is in the head, agreement is there and faith is there, allowing the man or woman to harvest into the earth realm what heaven had planted in the heart of the man.

Now pay close attention. Let's review what actually happened. Heaven sows the Word of God into the earth realm, into the heart of a man or woman where agreement is needed. At that time, the man's heart is not in agreement with heaven yet, but a process begins to take place in the heart that brings the heart, all by itself, into agreement with what was sown. Jesus uses a great illustration to show us this process. Comparing this process to a farmer sowing seed and how the plant matures, Jesus give us a picture of what faith looks like. In the natural realm, when the seed in the head is mature, it will look **EXACTLY** like the seed that was sown into the ground. Let me say that again.

When the seed that is in the head of the plant matures, it will look exactly—EXACTLY—like the seed that was sown into the ground.

Plant a corn plant and the mature seed in the ear will match the seed that you planted. They are the same, look the same, and taste the same. You cannot tell the difference between the two; they are identical. So let me paraphrase what Jesus is saying. When we hear the Word (Romans 10:17), we are actually scattering God's Word into our spirit men, our hearts. If we keep that Word in our hearts, it will mature; and when it is mature, the pictures in our hearts (the earth realm) will match what heaven says.

If we put it in different terms, we could say that as you sow a promise from heaven into your heart, it will slowly produce confidence of what God said all by itself. Eventually, your heart will be fully persuaded of what heaven says, and agreement will be there. For instance, if you are facing sickness, your circumstances in your body are speaking to you that you are sick. As you sow the Word of God that says that God has paid the price for your healing through what Jesus did, your heart slowly begins to become convinced of what God says all by itself.

When that word matures in your heart, the confidence that you are healed becomes what **you** believe and say. No longer are you simply quoting what heaven says. Your heart is now firmly convinced. When you say, "I am healed," it is not a formula that you are quoting; rather, this is what you believe and know to be a fact. What heaven says has now become your own perception of reality.

This is why Hebrews 11:1 (EHV) says:

> *Faith is being sure about what we hope for, being convinced about things we do not see.*

There is a supernatural assurance of what heaven says when faith is there, yet there is still another step in the process.

The man now must put in his sickle to harvest, to bring into his actual realm of existence, what he is sure of in his heart.

> *As soon as the grain is ripe,* ***he puts the sickle to it****, because the harvest has come.*
>
> —Mark 4:29

Notice that even though the heart is in agreement with heaven, and heaven's reality has become the man or woman's reality, no real change has yet occurred in the physical realm. Because man is the one who naturally has jurisdiction here in the earth, he is the one who must also release that authority of heaven into this realm. God cannot do it without the man or woman. I can show you this in the very familiar Scripture that we discussed earlier.

> *For with the heart one believes and is* ***justified****, and with the mouth one* ***confesses*** *and is saved.*
>
> —Romans 10:10 (ESV)

With the heart man believes the Word, producing faith, and is justified. Justify is a legal term meaning the administration of law. So when a man's heart is in agreement with heaven, and his heart is fully persuaded of what heaven says, he is justified. It is now legal for heaven to flow into his life, into the earth realm. But being justified alone does not release the power of God. Like a house that has the power run to the house from the power station, there is one more step—turning the switch on to release the power, and then the lights come on. Why? Because as Romans 10:10 points out, there is one more step after being justified.

A man or woman who stands before heaven and earth justified must then confess or act upon that agreement to actually release the power and anointing of God into the earth realm. Please read that Scripture again and then again until you completely understand what I am saying. This is how it works! This is how heaven gains legality in the earth realm—the heart is the interface of heaven in the earth realm, and then our words and actions are the switches that actually release heaven's power. Please pay close attention to the second part of that verse again: We are the ones who must release heaven's authority here.

The concept of heaven waiting on a man or woman to, first of all, provide legality and, secondly, jurisdiction in the earth realm can be seen through what Jesus taught in Matthew 16:19 and Matthew 18:18.

> *I will give you the keys of the kingdom of heaven; whatever you bind on earth will be bound in heaven, and whatever you loose on earth will be loosed in heaven.*
>
> —Matthew 16:19

Truly, I say to you, whatever you bind on earth shall be bound in heaven, and whatever you loose on earth shall be loosed in heaven.

—Matthew 18:18 (ESV)

Jesus states in Matthew 16:19 that He is going to give the church the keys (authority) of the Kingdom of heaven in the earth realm. He said that whatsoever you bind on earth, heaven will back up, and whatsoever you loose on earth, heaven will back up. Again, think of a police officer; he has the authority, but the government has the power. The police officer holds the key or the authority of the government, as he was sworn in to be an agent of that government. What he says, the government backs up. Remember, only a man or woman has legal jurisdiction here, and thus only a man or woman can give heaven legal jurisdiction here.

THIS IS HOW HEAVEN GAINS LEGALITY IN THE EARTH REALM—THE HEART IS THE INTERFACE OF HEAVEN IN THE EARTH REALM, AND THEN OUR WORDS AND ACTIONS ARE THE SWITCHES THAT ACTUALLY RELEASE HEAVEN'S POWER.

There is one more very important point that you need to know about faith. Let me reference our Scripture in Mark chapter 4 again for a moment.

*All by itself the **soil produces grain**—first the stalk, then the head, then the full kernel in the head.*

—Mark 4:28

Remember, Jesus defined the soil mentioned in this parable as representing the heart of man, or the spirit of man, as I mentioned before. Notice where faith is produced; does that surprise you? It is not a product of heaven, as most people believe, but it is produced here in the earth realm and is a product of your heart. You cannot pray for it or ask God for it. Faith is not needed in heaven. We will not need agreement in heaven. No, it is only required here in the earth realm, and it can only occur in the hearts of men and women on the earth. As the parable in Mark 4 teaches, there is only one way to get it—by putting the Word of God in your heart and letting the process of agreement take place. So if I need faith, what would I do? I would scatter the Word of God into my heart and let it grow until faith was there. That is the only way it comes.

Before I leave Mark 4, I want to talk about the sickle mentioned there again.

> *As soon as the grain is ripe,* ***he puts the sickle to it****, because the harvest has come.*
>
> —Mark 4:29

I believe that most of the church world has not been taught how to use the sickle, meaning they have not been taught how to harvest what they need. The church in general has been taught how to give but not how to cultivate and harvest from the seed they have sown. Jesus is very specific in this verse, saying that when the harvest of our faith is available, WE must put in the sickle. Even though we may have done a great job of releasing our seed in faith, unless we know how to put in the sickle, there will be no harvest. Quite frankly, I knew nothing about this either until the

Lord began teaching me how the Kingdom operates. Let me give you a few examples of what this looks like.

I was invited to speak at a church in Atlanta. It was a Wednesday night service, and the church was not that big, but that was fine with me. I just loved teaching people about the Kingdom. As I arrived at the church, I found it strange that the doors were locked and no one was there. It was ten minutes before service was to begin. I heard a really loud truck behind me; it sounded like it had no muffler at all. As I looked over, I saw an old beat-up, broken-down pickup truck pulling into the alley behind the church. I thought nothing of it; after all, I was in downtown Atlanta. As I waited, a man came walking from behind the building and introduced himself as the pastor. He said he was sorry for being late, but his old truck would not start. He told me he had to start the truck by coasting it downhill then, once getting up some speed, popping the clutch since the starter was inoperative. He said many times it would not start at all, and he would have to walk the five miles to the church.

As he went on telling me about his church, he told me that although he was the pastor of the church, the church's main function was to feed inner city people. They fed over 10,000 meals a month at that location.

As the pastor was speaking, I was getting upset. Here was a man of God who was feeding 10,000 people a month, and he did not even have a reliable car? He was the only picture of God that many of those people he fed would ever see. If they saw him barely making it, having to walk to church five miles on a 100-degree summer day, what confidence would they have that God could help them? I could take care of that. I had a fairly young car with 20,000 miles on it at home that I could give him. I told him of my plan and that I would send one of my staff down to Atlanta with the car. He, of course, was thrilled. I spent that night teaching him and his small church about the Kingdom of God and how it functioned in relation to money.

When I went home, I arranged for the car to be driven to Atlanta. When my staff member came to my house to pick up the car, I knew that I was making a spiritual transaction in heaven. I knew that as I released that car into the Kingdom of God, I could believe God for a vehicle that I would have need of as well. I am not a car person, meaning I am not really into cars. Some people are, but I am not. A car is just a tool to me. I like to have a nice car, of course, but I usually drive them until they need replaced.

When my staff member stopped by, I went out into my garage, and I laid my hands on that car and said, "Father, I release this car into the work of your ministry, and as I release this car, I receive back a car…." I hesitated. I know how specific the Kingdom of God is, and I knew that just the word "car" would not do. I also knew that I had to be specific and that Drenda and I needed to be in agreement concerning the specifics of what we received. As I stood there mid-sentence, I also realized that I had no idea what kind of car I wanted. So I started over, "Lord, today I release this car into your ministry, and I believe that I receive a really nice car as I sow, but I will have to get back to you on the model and type when I figure that out." That was it; the car was gone. I really did not have any car in mind that I could say, "Yes, I want THAT car."

A few months went by. Of course, Drenda was in agreement with me in giving the car away, and, like me, she did not have a clue what kind of car she wanted. Over the next two months, we talked about cars, and finally one day she said, "You know, I think I would enjoy having a convertible." I told her that I agreed and said

I thought that sounded fun, but what kind? Again, we did not even know what kind of convertibles were out there.

But one day as we were driving out to lunch, my wife suddenly said, "That's it!" "What's it?" I said. "That's it," she said as she was pointing across the parking lot of the restaurant we had pulled into. "What's it?" I said. "That car, that's the car I want!" I then saw a sharp convertible across the parking lot. "Let's go see what kind it is," I said. So we drove over to the car and pulled up behind it. Well, no wonder we liked it. It was a BMW 645Ci, a nice convertible for sure, and a very expensive one at that. To be honest with you, when I saw that make of car, I thought, *Okay, Lord, show us what to do.* I knew I was not going to pay $115,000 for a new BMW, but I also knew that God can do amazing things. Drenda and I did not tell anyone about the car or mention to anyone that we were looking for a car.

About two weeks later, Drenda's brother called us and said, "I found Drenda's car!" "What do you mean you found Drenda's car?" I said. He said, "I saw this car for sale, and all of a sudden, I just felt that this was supposed to be Drenda's car; and I was supposed to tell you about it." "What kind of car is it?" I asked. "It is a BMW 645Ci, and it is perfect; I mean perfect. It is a couple of years old, low mileage, and there is not a scratch on it. Besides that, you know the man who is selling it." "I do?" I said. "Yes. He said you should call him about it." Well, when he told me the car's make and model, knowing that it was the exact car that Drenda and I had said we both liked just a couple of weeks previously, I knew that God was up to something.

I called the man who owned the car. Yes, I did know him, and we talked a bit about the car, and he was telling me how great of a shape the car was in. And then he said these words to me. "You know, ever since we have been on the phone speaking about this car, I just really feel like this is supposed to be Drenda's car." I had not even mentioned to him that I was looking at the car for Drenda. The man went on and said, "I tell you what I am going to do. I am going to sell it to you for $28,000." I could hardly believe what my ears were hearing. The car was worth so much more than that. When I told Drenda about it, she was thrilled, to say the least. We paid cash for that car and still have it today. It still runs and looks great. There is still not a scratch on it, and we have taken many drives in that car with the top down, the stereo blaring, and the sun breathing life into a tired day.

Our favorite trip was driving that awesome convertible through the Colorado mountains, with our camping supplies in the trunk. Our daughter Kirsten was with us on that trip, and I remember driving through Kansas on I-70 during the night with the top down. Kirsten was lying in the back asleep as I drove. The stars shone so brightly over our heads, and the road was vacant except for an occasional truck or two. It was one of those perfect nights where the air was just right and all was wonderful in the world. We spent the next two weeks driving through the Rockies, and I found out just how great that car handled. One word can describe it—awesome!

But here is the one million-dollar question. How did that car get here? Why was it the exact car that Drenda said, "That's it!" about? I knew that the Kingdom of God brought that car into our lives. I knew that when I sowed that car to that pastor, I was putting spiritual law into place. I remember saying that I was receiving back a car, not an SUV, not a jeep, a car; I remember saying a nice one. But Drenda and I had to put the sickle in. That car would not have shown up until we said, "That's it!" Although I was in faith when I released that car, we had not put in the sickle until Drenda said, "That's it."

Another incident happened that brought out this principle in an even greater way. As I said, I like to hunt. I live in some very good hunting country, and I am blessed to own my own hunting land. On my over 55 acres, I have about 20 acres of hardwoods and about 10 to 12 acres of marsh. I hunt deer and squirrel every year with great success. There are always ducks and geese flying around, but for some reason, I never really thought about hunting them. Oh, once or twice over the years, the boys and I walked down to the marsh and jumped up a few geese for supper. But we never truly duck hunted.

Well, a few years ago, as I watched dozens and dozens of ducks flying into the marsh, I thought that I would try some duck hunting. Wow, it was so exciting! I was hooked. During that fall's duck hunting, I found out that I needed some serious practice shooting at ducks. I managed to bag a few and found that they were very good to eat as well. I noticed that many times the ducks were just out of range or on the edge of my shotgun's range, which I believed contributed to some of my misses. I was using my regular, all-around shotgun that I used for everything from rabbits to deer, a Remington model 11-87. Don't misunderstand, I love that gun, and it is a great gun. But I had heard there were new gun models that were made just for duck hunting. They were camouflaged and were chambered for three and a half inch magnum shells, which I knew would help on those long passing shots. I planned to look into one of them before the next duck season began.

Well, the duck season was over, it was then January, and I was walking through Cabela's and thought I would walk through the shotgun section to see what those guns looked like. As I walked into the shotgun section, I saw that they had a whole section just for shotguns dedicated to duck hunting. I looked at a few of them and thought about buying the one I liked, but it was $2,000 and the duck hunting season was months away. *I'll wait*, I thought to myself. But I did something unusual as I was about to leave. I really did not realize what I was doing when I did it. I just did it without thinking. I pointed at the shotgun I wanted and said out loud. "I'll have that gun, in the name of Jesus." Again, I did not think much about it; I was just making a declaration that I was going to have that gun. My heart had a clear picture of the duck gun I wanted.

I was invited to speak at a business conference a couple of weeks later, and something happened there that caught my attention. After I spoke, the owner of the company walked up and said they had wanted to get me a gift in appreciation of my coming. He said, "We knew you like to hunt, so we bought you this shotgun." I was in shock as they brought out a brand-new, Benelli, semi-automatic duck gun, the exact one I had seen in the store, the one to which I had pointed! Are you seeing this? How did that exact gun show up? I had given dozens of guns away over the years but had never put in the sickle. In other words, I had sown those guns in faith and generosity but had never put in the sickle. I had never said, "Lord, that's it! That's the one I want." But the minute I did, the harvest showed up!

I was relating the story of the shotgun to a fellow minister friend of mine. He said, "Yes, I suppose God does that sometimes. He will just bless you with a special little gift to

...GOD JUST WANTED TO SHOW ME HE LOVED ME. HE SHOWED ME HE LOVED ME WHEN HE SENT JESUS FOR ME AND GAVE ME THE KINGDOM!

tell you He loves you." As I thought about what he said, I realized, "No, that is not right. Yes, God loves me, but He did not just want to surprise me with a little gift." The car and the gun had come not because God just wanted to show me He loved me. He showed me He loved me when He sent Jesus for me and gave me the Kingdom!

I have said for years that the church has done a fairly great job of teaching about giving but a horrible job of teaching people how to harvest. So can you tell what the sickle is from the preceding stories? I hope it is obvious! The sickle is our words!

> *The tongue has the power of life and death, and those who love it will eat its fruit.*
>
> —Proverb 18:21

There was a season where the church seemed to teach a lot about our confession. I have been with people, and you may have also, that would say something and then cover their mouths and say, "I need to watch my confession." That sounds like a noble task, and I agree that will help keep the Word in your heart. However, watching your confession really has nothing to do with the sickle. What? But I thought you just said the sickle was our words. Yes, I did, but just mastering the formula of saying the right thing is not the key by itself.

> *Truly, I say to you, whoever **says** to this mountain, "Be taken up and thrown into the sea," and does not doubt in his heart, but **believes** that what **he says** will come to pass, it will be done for him.*
>
> —Mark 11:23 (ESV)

Again, the sickle in Mark chapter 4 is your words! By the time Mark chapter 4 discusses the sickle, it has already discussed the process of faith and how to get it. It says when the seed is mature, you put in the sickle because the harvest has come. The harvest has come because you are in faith, agreeing with heaven in your heart. The above verse in Mark 11 bears out the same principle. Your heart believes the Word, then you speak and release heaven's authority. But notice the phrase, "*believes that what he says will come to pass.*" The test of faith is if you believe what you are saying. Just saying or confessing the Word of God is not faith by itself. Unless your heart is in agreement with heaven, you can confess until you are blue in the face and nothing will happen. So should your monitor your confession or your heart?

> *The good person brings what is good out of the good stored up in his heart, and the evil person brings what is evil out of the evil within. To be sure, what his mouth speaks flows from the heart.*
>
> —Luke 6:45 (EHV)

> *Above all else, guard your heart, for it is the wellspring of life. Put away perversity from your mouth; keep corrupt talk far from your lips.*
>
> —Proverbs 4:23-24 (BSB)

We can clearly see that what we say comes out of our hearts and what we believe. By following the process in Mark chapter 4, we know how to actually change what our hearts believe and bring them into alignment with heaven and in faith. Then when we are fully persuaded, we put the sickle in with our words and action.

Got it? Great, let's move on.

As we continue our discussion on faith, I want to bring up a question that you must be able to answer.

How do I know if I am actually in faith?

That is a great question and one you **<u>must</u>** know since it is impossible to pray the prayer of faith without first being in faith. There are many ways to know if you are in faith or not, many symptoms that you need to know and to look for. You can make a lot of bad fear-based decisions when you are not in faith. Fear-based decisions will always hold you hostage to the earth curse and will cause you to miss out on what God wants for you.

So, what is the evidence of being in faith? The first sign is easy; you can look back at our definition of faith and understand that being fully persuaded in your heart is a real key. But many times we think we are persuaded but are only agreeing in our minds with the Word and not in our hearts. You need to be able to tell the difference. When you are fully persuaded, there is, of course, a mental agreement with what the Word says but also a knowing of being sure, a confidence that brings peace and expectation.

> *Faith is being sure about what we hope for, convinced about things we do not see.*
>
> —Hebrews 11:1 (EHV)

If you had evidence that you had something, would you still need to be reassured that you had it? Of course not. Again, when you are in faith, there is a knowing, a peace, and a confidence that you have what the Word of God says, even though you may not see it yet. Many people say it this way: "I know that I know that I know that I know I have it." This knowing is from the inside and not from what circumstances are telling you. It is in your spirit man or your heart. Fear is gone, no more nagging thoughts of worry bombard your mind; you know it is done.

Another aspect of being in faith is joy and expectation. Your answer is here. You have it! Faith is more than a feeling of peace or confidence, although you will have that. You should also be able to defend your position spiritually. When I say that, think of a courtroom and you as the attorney cross-examining the witness. Why do you believe what you believe about your situation? How would you defend your position? There is only one answer, the Word of God.

For instance, if someone came to your house and said, "Hey, get out of my house," would you say, "Oh, I am sorry; give us a day, and we will be out"? No, you wouldn't; you would probably laugh. If the fellow said, "No, this is my house; get out or I will see you in court," your reply would be, "I will gladly see you in court!" At the hearing, you would calmly show the judge your deed. He would take one look at it and arrest the other guy for harassment and make him pay all court costs. Your confidence was established not on how you felt and your emotions but, rather, on the law and the fact that you legally owned the house.

When it comes to being in faith, I find that many times people who do not understand what faith is are easily confused by putting their confidence in their actions instead of their only source of faith, which is the Word of

> ***"FAITH IS BEING SURE ABOUT WHAT WE HOPE FOR, CONVINCED ABOUT THINGS WE DO NOT SEE."***
> **—HEBREWS 11:1 (EHV)**

God. It is easy to confuse the action or formula of acting on the Word of God with the real power of the Kingdom, which comes from a heart that is confidently persuaded. For instance, if you sowed money into the Kingdom of God, and I asked you why you believe you will receive a return on that giving, your answer should not be, "Because on such and such a date I gave a certain amount of money." That confession is looking only at your action, the formula, and has no anchor of assurance. Your assurance can only come from the Word of God.

I cannot count the number of people I have prayed with that when asked why they believe they will receive when I pray simply stare at me with no answer. When I ask, I am looking for their faith, their agreement with heaven. I want to hear them say, "I know I will receive because God has promised me in such and such book of the Bible and in such and such verse that it is mine." Chances are if they cannot give me a Scripture, they are not anchored and they really do not have a clue where their boat is going.

Remember, faith can only exist when you know the will of God. Why? Because faith can only exist when your heart is in agreement with the will of God. I believe that many people think they are in faith when they are not. Again, their minds may agree that the Word of God is true and good, but faith is there only when their hearts are fully persuaded. For many, their minds agree with the Word of God, but their hearts are not settled.

Here is a good illustration of what I am talking about, one which I believe will point out that many are not in faith when they think they are. What if I were to tell you that I had recently found out that the sky was not blue, as people said, but that the color blue as they called it was really the color yellow? In other words, I told you that we had been taught wrong all our lives about colors and that blue is not really blue but yellow. What would you do? Would you gasp in shock and quickly grab your cell phone and call your first grade teacher and yell at them, accusing them of messing up your life, teaching you all the colors wrong? I do not think so. There would be no emotional reaction of fear, no drama. You would simply know that I was an idiot, dismiss the comment as irrational, and go about your business. Why? Because you are fully persuaded that blue is blue!

Now, let's compare my example to our faith discussion. What if you were fully persuaded of what God said about healing, and a doctor told you that you were going to die of cancer? You would look at that doctor and think he was the idiot because you knew there was no way that could happen. Why? It's because you were fully persuaded of the healing provisions that Jesus paid for. Do you see it? Of course, many people pray, but upon examination, I find their prayers are not prayers of faith but of hope, with them unsure of the outcome. My friend, this is why it is so important that we build ourselves up with the Word of God. We need to know what God's will is so that we can be confident in what He says, and also so we can reject what is not His will. Let me give you an example from my own life which illustrates just how important it is to feed on what God says about life.

I was tired, as it had been a tough few weeks as a business owner (this was before I pastored a church). My schedule had been packed with sales calls and, of course, the financial pressure of living on commissions. I was going to my dentist for a routine filling. Everything was normal until the dentist went to inject the Novocain. As he inserted the needle, there was a sudden jolt, and then my jaw instantly went numb, as opposed to it slowly numbing up. I was surprised, and I told the dentist what had happened. He said, "Oh, I guess I hit the nerve." I quickly asked him, "Is that normal?" He said these words, "Well, it usually heals up." What? Did I hear him correctly? "Doctor, what do you mean it usually heals up?" He said, "Well, about 80 percent to 85 percent of the time, it completely heals up with no permanent negative effect."

What? Suddenly fear rose up in me. Now what? Is it going to heal up? My mind was starting to be consumed with fearful thoughts. After my appointment, my face stayed numb, unlike a normal dentist's appointment where the numbness slowly wears off. I was heading to a client's appointment about an hour away from the dentist's appointment, so I had plenty of time to think about what had just happened. But all the way to that appointment, I was in agony, not from any pain but from the lack of peace and from the fear that was swirling through my mind.

On the way home from the appointment, later in the day, I stopped at a friend's house. My face was still numb, and I was looking for some reassurance from someone that this thing would heal up. Notice my mistake: I did not look to the Word of God but to a person who was not even a strong believer for my confidence. I told this person what had happened and was waiting for their, "That's no big deal, Gary; it will heal up!" Instead, here is what I heard. "Oh, no! I had a friend who had that happen, and their face never healed. Their face has been paralyzed ever since." I could not believe what I was hearing! My mind was then in fear overdrive. I acted like I knew it would be okay and thanked him for his time.

AT THAT POINT, I KNEW THAT MY ONLY HOPE WAS THE WORD OF GOD.

In desperation, I stopped by another friend's home and asked the same question, and in shock, I heard the same reply, "Oh, no," they said, "I had a friend who had this happen, and their face never healed. Their face is still paralyzed today."

After this visit, I was undone. I knew that God heals (in my mind), but I just could not get rid of that fear. My heart was definitely not persuaded. That night, I was in agony! My mind was full of fear, and my face was still just as numb as it had been at the dentist's office. As I was trying to get to sleep, I began to feel a bit of pain under my right ear. Could it be? My dad had fought a battle with Bell's palsy a year or two earlier, and he had told me that it had started with some pain just under his ear. Bell's palsy occurs when the nerve that controls the facial muscles, which travels through a small hole in the bone just under the ear, becomes pinched by an infection or inflammation.

As I lay there trying to find sleep, all I could hear were these words going through my thoughts, "You are going to have Bell's palsy just like your dad." When I woke up in the morning, I had a full-blown case of Bell's palsy! Not only was my jaw numb, but also my entire face on the right side was numb, and I could not close my eyes or my mouth. I was a mess.

I went to a local doctor to confirm my suspicions. After the examination, he looked at me and said that I indeed had a full-blown case of Bell's palsy. I then said, "What happens next?" He said, "Well, in about 80 to 85 percent of the cases, it will heal up without permanent paralysis." "Did he say what I thought he just said?"

At that point, I knew that I was in trouble. I knew that the devil would not stop there, and I did not want to see what came next. I knew enough about spiritual warfare to realize I was heading in the wrong direction. Remember, this was years ago before I knew very much about these types of things. But I knew enough to realize that I had to tackle this thing spiritually if I was going to have any success at beating it. I also realized that this was a demonic setup to catch me off guard when I was tired and not anticipating any trouble.

At that point, I knew that my only hope was the Word of God. In myself, I had absolutely no ability to stop the fear that was plaguing my mind. So I wrote out 3 x 5 cards with healing Scriptures on them and posted them all over my house. I repented before the Lord and began the process of developing faith in my heart. I knew that I had to sow the Word in my heart for faith to develop, so I would meditate on the Word of God throughout the day.

At first, nothing changed. My face stayed numb, and I constantly fought the spirit of fear. After about a week, with still nothing changing in my face, it happened!

Just like the process our Scripture in Mark 4:26-28 teaches, as I sowed the Word into my heart, faith began to be formed, first the blade, then the stalk, the head, and then the mature grain in the head.

Throughout this entire process, there was not agreement and thus no faith—yet. However, even though I did not see change or know how this process works, according to our Scripture in Mark 4, things were indeed changing.

The change I am talking about is not in the manifested natural realm yet, but the change is occurring in our hearts. If we hold on to the Word, the Word slowly changes our hearts' belief system from one of unbelief to agreement with heaven all by itself.

So in this case, I held on to the Word, knowing that it was my only answer. Suddenly, one day, as I was walking through my house with all those 3 x 5 cards with healing Scriptures on them posted everywhere, I just happened to glance at one that I had seen a hundred times. But this time when I looked at it, BAM! Suddenly, the anointing came on me, fear instantly left, and I KNEW that I was healed. Yes, my face was still numb. There was no change, but I knew I was healed. Within a couple of hours, my face was completely normal, with all the numbness gone. Praise God! The Word works!

Even though I had allowed my spiritual life to weaken due to my neglect and busyness, I eventually realized my mistake and repented from my foolishness. This was way back when I was first learning how faith really worked, and I did not have a lot of experience in this area. I look back on what I did, asking people of my future when in trouble instead of going straight to the Word of God, as foolish. Once I understood what was going on, I did turn to the Word of God with confidence. Unfortunately, most people are not confident in this process because they have never been taught about faith and how it comes. Since they are unaware of the process, when they are under pressure, they let go of the Word, thinking it does not work.

Understand Satan's counterattack.

Christine came to our church not knowing much about God. She was born again in one of our Sunday morning services, and her life was radically changed. In our church, we have a Kingdom orientation class. One of the areas we talk and teach about is the legal right to receive healing. Christine had been having trouble with her hearing for years. In fact, she had been wearing a hearing aid for 40 years and had already lost over 50 percent of her hearing. Her mother was deaf, and her brother was also suffering from this same issue with loss of hearing. When Christine heard that, as a believer, she had a legal right to be healed, she was so excited!

In the class, my wife, Drenda, laid her hands on her and prayed for her hearing to be open, and instantly, pop, she could hear perfectly. Christine began screaming and crying and praising God. When Drenda and Christine came and told me the good news, I felt an urge to warn her about Satan's counterattack. I told Drenda to instruct Christine that if the symptoms started to come back for her to speak boldly to the issue and declare that she was healed and for Satan to back off. The next morning, the test came. Her hearing had reverted back to her inability to hear well. So, she did exactly what we said, "NO! Satan, I am not receiving this. I am healed, and I *was* healed, in the name of Jesus!" Pop! Her ears popped opened, and they have stayed open ever since.

Remember that Satan will counterattack and try to retake territory. Don't let him do it. Stand on the Word of God!

In this appendix, I have taken some time to give you a basic understanding of what faith is, how it functions, how to know if you are in faith, and where to get faith. For the Kingdom of God to operate in your life, you have to know this. Remember, Jesus told the woman that received her healing in Matthew 9:20-22, "*Your faith has healed you.*" And so shall it be for you: Your faith, your heart being fully convinced of what heaven says, and putting in the sickle will be your answer for any problem or need you may face in life.[29]

---

29 The teaching in the Faith Appendix was taken from my *Your Financial Revolution: The Power of Allegiance* book.

All of my material is available at garykeesee.com.

If you would like information about my company, you can reach Forward Financial Group at forwardfinancialgroup.com or 1-(800)-815-0818.

If you would like information on how to invest your retirement money with no risk of principal decline due to market swings, or if you are looking for a way to maximize your retirement income, again, reach out to Forward Financial Group.

If you are interested in hosting one of our Financial Revolution Conferences at your church, please reach out to our office for information.

Again, our office number is 1-(800)-815-0818.

Gary and Drenda Keesee Ministries
P.O. Box 779
New Albany, Ohio 43054